Time Pieces

A DUBLIN MEMOIR

Time Pieces

A DUBLIN MEMOIR

JOHN BANVILLE

Photographs by Paul Joyce

HACHETTE
BOOKS
IRELAND

First published in 2016 by Hachette Books Ireland

Text © John Banville, 2016
Photographs © Paul Joyce, 2016

A CIP catalogue record for this title is available from the British Library.

ISBN 978 1 473 61904 3

Book design and typesetting by Anú Design
Printed and bound in Italy by Graphicom

Hachette Books Ireland policy is to use papers that are natural, renewable and recyclable and made from wood grown in sustainable forests. The logging and manufacturing processes are expected to conform to the environmental regulations of the country of origin.

Hachette Books Ireland
8 Castlecourt Centre
Castleknock
Dublin 15, Ireland

A division of Hachette UK Ltd
Carmelite House, Victoria Embankment,
London EC4Y 0DZ
www.hachettebooksireland.ie

To Harry Crosbie, OBE

Contents

1

About Time

DUBLIN WAS NEVER MY DUBLIN, which made it all
the more alluring. I was born in Wexford, a small town
that was smaller and more remote then, sequestered in
its own past. My birthday falls on 8 December, the Feast of the
Immaculate Conception—I have always taken this as an example
of how laughably imprecise in the matter of birth-dates bungling
Heaven can be. The eighth used to be both a Holy Day and a
public holiday, when people from the provinces flocked to
the capital to do their Christmas shopping and marvel at the
Christmas lights. So my birthday treat on successive years in the
first half of the 1950s was a trip by train to Dublin, a thing I looked
forward to for months beforehand—indeed, I suspect I began to

look forward to next year's jaunt the moment that year's had ended.

We would leave from the town's North Station in the wintry darkness of early morning. I believe there were still steam trains then, although diesel was the coming thing. How thrilling it was to walk through the sombre, deserted streets, my head still fuzzy from sleep, with the long day's adventure all before me. The train would arrive from Rosslare Harbour, carrying blear-eyed passengers off the overnight ferry from Fishguard in Wales, half of them drunk and the other half still showing the effects of sea-sickness. Away we would chug, the window beside me a black glass mirror in which I could study my menacingly shadowed reflection and imagine myself a confidential agent—as spies used to be called in the espionage novels of a previous age—on board the Orient Express and bound on a top-secret mission to the dusky and dangerous East.

We would have been somewhere in the approaches to Arklow when the dawn came up, turning the frost-white fields to a shade of sharply glistening mica-pink.

Certain moments in certain places, apparently insignificant, imprint themselves on the memory with improbable vividness and clarity—improbable because, so clear and so vivid are they, the suspicion arises that one's fancy must have made them up: that one must, in a word, have imagined them. Of those December journeys I recall, or am convinced I recall, a certain spot where the train slowed at a river bend—the Avoca river, it must have been—a spot I can still see clearly in my memory's eye, and which I have returned to repeatedly in my novels, as here, for instance, in *The Newton Letter*:

Beyond the river a flat field ran to the edge of a wooded hill, and at the foot of the hill there was a house, not very big, solitary and square, with a steep roof. I would gaze at that silent house and wonder, in a hunger of curiosity, what lives were lived there. Who stacked that firewood, hung that holly wreath, left those tracks in the hoarfrost on the hill? I can't express the odd aching pleasure of that moment. I knew, of course, that those hidden lives wouldn't be much different from my own. But that was the point. It wasn't the exotic I was after, but the *ordinary*, that strangest and most elusive of enigmas.

Dublin, of course, was the opposite of ordinary. Dublin was for me what Moscow was for Irina in Chekhov's *Three Sisters*, a place of magical promise towards which my starved young soul endlessly yearned. I was luckier than Irina in that the journey from Wexford to Dublin was relatively short, and I got to make it with satisfying frequency. That the city itself, the real Dublin, was, in those poverty-stricken 1950s, mostly a grey and graceless place did not mar my dream of it—and I dreamed of it even when I was present in it, so that mundane reality was being constantly transformed before my eyes into high romance; there is no one more romantic than a small boy, as Robert Louis Stevenson knew better than most.

• • • • •

When does the past become the past? How much time must elapse before what merely happened begins to give off the mysterious, numinous glow that is the mark of true pastness? After all, the resplendent vision we carry with us in memory was once merely the present, dull and workaday and wholly unremarkable, except in those moments when one has just fallen in love, say, or won the lottery, or has been delivered bad news by the doctor. What is the magic that is worked upon experience, when it is consigned to the laboratory of the past, there to be shaped and burnished to a finished radiance? These questions, which are all only one question, have fascinated me since when, as a child, I first came to the tremendous discovery that creation consisted not just of me and my appurtenances—mother, hunger, a preference for dryness over wetness—but of me on one side and on the other of *the world*: the world of other people, other phenomena, other things.

Let us say, the present is where we live, while the past is where we dream. Yet if it is a dream, it is substantial, and sustaining. The past buoys us up, a tethered and ever-expanding hot-air balloon.

And yet, I ask again, what is it? What transmutation must the present go through in order to become the past? Time's alchemy works in a bright abyss.

· · · · ·

Westland Row Station—it did not become Pearse Station until

years later—was mostly a vast soot-blackened glass dome, a couple of grim platforms, and a ramp leading down to the street. It seems to me now that on every one of those eighths of December we arrived in rain. This was not the driving, pounding rain of the provinces, but a special urban variety, its drops as fine and as penetrating as neutrinos, those teeming showers of subatomic, indeed sub-subatomic, particles that flash through you and me and all things at every instant. This rain did not so much make the pavements wet as turn them greasy, so that one had to make one's way over them with caution in one's slippery leather soles.

At the station exit we turned left on to Westland Row, and were at once loomed over by what seems to me one of the city's most oddly placed churches, St Andrew's, rammed as if by a celestial pile-driver into the middle of a terrace of unassuming and resolutely secular eighteenth-century houses. The building always appeared to me slightly demented, and still so appears, with its pair of outsized mock-Corinthian pillars, its huge unwelcoming door, and its shallowly pitched roof on the apex of which there stands a statue of St Andrew himself, older brother of the more famous Peter, gesticulating in frozen frustration, waving his arms in what seems an unheeded warning of imminent apocalypse.[*]

At the top of the street there was, and is, Kennedys pub, where Samuel Beckett used to drink when he was an undergraduate at

---

[*] In her essential Pevsner architectural guide to Dublin, Christine Casey trenchantly observes of St Andrew's: 'Few buildings in Dublin so tangibly evoke Catholic middle-class aspirations in the wake of Emancipation.'

nearby Trinity College. Turning left and immediately right, we would come up into Merrion Square, where, at number one, a fine example, at least in its exterior, of a terraced Georgian townhouse, Oscar Wilde was born, to William Wilde, an 'eminent physician', as they used to say. Oscar's mother was the remarkable and fascinating Jane Francesca Wilde, née Elgee, who in the 1840s wrote patriotic poems for the Young Irelander newspaper *The Nation* under the pen-name Speranza; so stirring were her verses that at one turbulent time she came very close to being sent to jail on a charge of sedition.

I need hardly say I knew none of these things at the time of which I am writing. I doubt I had even heard of poor Oscar, who today is commemorated by a hideous and garishly painted statue, representing him indecorously asprawl on a rock behind railings at the corner of the square opposite his birthplace. What indignities we consider ourselves free to visit upon the famous dead! We have named a gunship after Samuel Beckett, that most peace-loving of men, and scraps of prose from *Ulysses* are embossed on miniature brass plates set into Dublin pavements for everyone to tread upon.

Here I pause to reflect in wonderment how remarkably things chime with each other, however faintly, across the centuries. Jane 'Speranza' Wilde's father was a Wexford solicitor, and not long ago I stayed in the hotel room in Paris where her son Oscar, weighed down by his debts and bemoaning the awfulness of the wallpaper, breathed his last. For such a large place, the world does sometimes seem suspiciously small.

In the time of my earliest birthday jaunts my Aunt Nan, my

mother's sister, who lived all her adult life in Dublin, occupied a tiny flat in Percy Place.* It was on the ground floor of a house that is long gone now; the feature of it I recall most clearly is that just inside the front door one had to take a steep step down from the footpath into the hallway, a manoeuvre I always found alarming, even when I had grown big enough to manage it with ease. Childhood is fraught with obscure fears and frights.

In the upstairs flat—in those days they were always flats, never apartments, no matter how spacious or grand they might be—lived a large and raucous family named, peculiarly, and fascinatingly, I thought, Reck. One of the Reck children, a tomboyish girl with ringlets and bony pink knees, was the first unrequited love of my life. I used to dally longingly in the dingy hallway, with its smell of stewed tea and the stink of 'slops', hoping for a glimpse of the inviolable beloved as she came thundering down the stairs in her big school shoes, her ringlets bouncing. I doubt she even noticed me, lurking there ashen-faced in inarticulate yearning, one of Cupid's more precocious casualties.

On the other side of the street there was a terrace of half a dozen houses, which must have been newly built at that period; middle-class abodes, they were, with bay windows and gleaming

---

* I always coveted number two Percy Place, a little brick house hard by Huband Bridge, overlooking the canal lock and shaded by an exquisite weeping willow. Lately I discovered that the house and two others were built by William Beckett, father of Samuel, and that Samuel and his brother Frank jointly inherited the three houses—it seems the deeds to number two, at least, bore the names of the brothers up until the 1970s. Well, well . . .

brass door-knockers. Norman Sherry, in his gargantuan biography of Graham Greene, relates a curious anecdote concerning that otherwise respectable and proper-seeming terrace. Some time in the early 1950s, Greene's American-born lover, the beautiful and racy Catherine Walston, wife of Lord Harry Walston, a fabulously wealthy English businessman, came and lodged for a time at one of those houses, and while she was there kept a cushion stuffed under her dress to give the impression that she was pregnant. It seems the reason was that one of her husband's girlfriends was in Ireland and expecting a child, and Catherine, being the good sport that she was, had agreed to pretend the inconvenient babe was hers. She came over to Dublin, displaying her prominent fake bump, to attend the birth in secret and bring the little boy back to England as if he were her own son. *Autres temps, autres moeurs.*

I think it was at this time, too, that Lady Walston, who according to one of her lovers 'had a thing for priests', met Father Donal O'Sullivan, a colourful Jesuit who would become director of the Arts Council, and whom Greene, green with jealousy, nicknamed 'Skunkburgh'. Catherine and the reverend father had an affair, or something very like it—the sexual arrangements of those days, when contraceptives were banned by law in Ireland, hardly bear speculating upon. Certainly the couple took annual holidays together in Venice, and are reported to have had frequent trysts at her Dublin flat—in Percy Place? I do hope so.

I wonder if, during her time here, Lady Walston encountered another louche priest-about-town, Father Con Lee, a curate at that

spireless but aspiring St Andrew's in Westland Row. He was a dashing fellow who wore exceptionally well-cut clerical suits—his full name was Cornelius Frawley Lee and his family owned Frawley's, a once popular and highly successful department store in Thomas Street—smoked cigarettes in an ebony holder, and sported a pearl-handled cane. My sister knew him, and tells me that the street children in Westland Row had nicknamed him Bat Masterson, presumably for his dark and dashing dandyism. He fancied himself something of a literary type—he makes a fleeting appearance in the memoirs of the poet John Montague, who records the irreverent reverend calling in of an evening on him and his wife in their Herbert Place flat. He was the first Catholic chaplain at Trinity College Dublin. Archbishop John Charles McQuaid, of execrated memory, summoned him to the Archbishop's Palace and informed him of the appointment, adding menacingly that it was an unofficial posting and that if there was 'trouble', of what kind he did not specify, Father Lee was 'on his own'. Con Lee was just the sort of fellow Catherine Walston would have been pleased to add to her collection of questionable clerics.

How odd it is to think that I might have on occasion and all unknowingly glimpsed La Walston, with her cushion under her frock, as I was about to take that deep step down into the hallway of my Aunt Nan's flat in Percy Place.

My mother and my sister and I—I don't think my father accompanied us on those birthday outings—would arrive in Percy Place at mid-morning, bedraggled after the journey, drenched with rain and smelling like sheep. Aunt Nan would have prepared a birthday breakfast treat—the word 'brunch' had not yet been foisted upon the language—of sausages, rashers, fried egg and fried bread, washed down with cups of teak-coloured tea, strong enough, as my mother would say, to trot a mouse on. There would also be a chocolate cream cake from the Kylemore Bakery, with my name piped on to it in white icing.

My aunt was a spinster, a term still current then—I always preferred the more genteel-sounding 'maiden lady'—and even yet I do not care, or dare, to dwell overmuch on what must have been the sadness of her solitary life, which I did nothing to alleviate when later, in the early 1960s, I shared another flat with her, round the corner, on Upper Mount Street. Mind you, Aunt Nan's manner was anything but sad: she had a subversive sense of humour, and regarded with chuckling scorn all those set in authority over us huddled masses. As I recall, she nursed a particular smouldering contempt for our Taoiseach, or prime minister, of the day, Éamon de Valera—'Dev'—erstwhile leader of the dominant Fianna Fáil party and a veteran of the 1916 Rising, whose American citizenship had, unfortunately, according to not a few of his political opponents, saved him from the firing squad. As to what it was exactly that Dev had done to earn my aunt's contumely I cannot say, but I do recall clearly the way her lip would curl when she uttered the name of 'that long streak of misery'.

Toy guns. I had a passion for toy guns. Early on I did an inventory of my arsenal and came up with twenty-four assorted six-shooters, automatics, 'ray-guns', mock Smith & Wesson Saturday Night

Specials, derringers, flintlocks and, my favourite, a miniature but carefully detailed version of the famous Winchester '73 rifle, with which, in the 1950 Western named after it, Lin McAdam (James Stewart) finally nailed 'Dutch Henry' Brown (Stephen McNally), before settling down with his true love, Lola, the saloon girl (Shelley Winters, another of my early hopeless loves). Queasy after too many slices of Kylemore cake, but greatly excited all the same, I would tear open Aunt Nan's present, which invariably would be a toy weapon of some kind—although one year she gave me a plastic submarine I could sail in the bath, and which was a great success, even if it was not the hoped-for gat.

After our late breakfast came the excursion 'into town'. I imagine we would have taken the number 10 bus from Baggot Street to the city centre.

Caught, I pause a moment in memory on Baggot Street Bridge and consider the view northwards—is it northwards?—along the Grand Canal to Huband Bridge and beyond. I imagine we all have a particular place that is a kind of private Paradise, the Heaven we should wish to go to after death, if go somewhere we must. For me, that stretch of placid water, rustling reeds and dark-umber towpath from Baggot Street down to Lower Mount Street is the loveliest aquascape I know of, trumping even that other Canale Grande, the one with the warbling gondoliers. I consider it among the happier blessings of my life that I was allowed from earliest days to come to know that area, 'Baggotonia', as its denizens fondly and proprietorially called it, and that eventually I would have the

surpassing good luck to live there, during a number of what I suppose I must regard as my 'formative years'.

Yes, I know, Patrick Kavanagh had a prior claim to the canal, which I happily concede to his shade. I intended here to quote a fragment from the opening of his most famous poem on the subject, but when I re-read it I found it to be such a lovely thing that I decided I must copy it out in full.

Lines Written on a Seat on the Grand Canal, Dublin
'Erected to the memory of Mrs Dermot O'Brien'

O commemorate me where there is water,
Canal water, preferably, so stilly
Greeny at the heart of summer. Brother
Commemorate me thus beautifully
Where by a lock Niagarously roars
The falls for those who sit in the tremendous silence
Of mid-July. No one will speak in prose
Who finds his way to these Parnassian islands.
A swan goes by head low with many apologies,
Fantastic light looks through the eyes of bridges—
And look! a barge comes bringing from Athy
And other far-flung towns mythologies.
O commemorate me with no hero-courageous
Tomb—just a canal-bank seat for the passer-by.

The poet got his heavily hinted-at wish—in fact, it was granted him twice over, for there are not one but two seats by the canal dedicated to his memory, which would surely have elicited a gratified grin from the crusty old codger.

The idea of erecting a memorial seat was first conceived in 1967 by the late John Ryan, artist, magazine editor, critic and most unlikely publican—he owned the Bailey, a fashionably 'arty' pub and eating place in Duke Street that is flourishing still—who was a figure of some moment in his time. As he relates in his Dublin memoir *Remembering How We Stood*—given the drinking habits of the people he writes about, a more accurate title, some wag observed, would have been *Forgetting How We Staggered*—Ryan and his friend Denis Dwyer set up a committee with the aim of erecting a memorial seat. The committee met, rather oddly, on Sunday mornings, in the Ormond, 'that hotel of shimmering and fugal Joycean memories', as Ryan wrote. Fearing the inevitable 'split', which as Brendan Behan said was always the first item on the agenda of any Irish political or social movement, Ryan and his colleagues gave themselves a deadline of 17 March 1968. 'The Irish can only work to deadlines,' Ryan observed. 'In the vapidness of unlimited time, their hopes and aspirations dissolve like the mists of the morning.'

The seat was designed by the artist Michael Farrell, 'basing his scheme on a rough sketch I had done on a drip-mat on the bar of the Bailey', according to Ryan. It was made of oak wood from County Meath and granite from the Dublin mountains, and lines from Kavanagh's poem were inscribed in the stone by the monumental

sculptor John Cullen. The materials and manufacture were paid for by subscriptions from, among others, the English poet John Heath-Stubbs, the future President of Ireland Cearbhall Ó Dálaigh, and Dr George Otto Simms, the Protestant Archbishop of Dublin. Kavanagh's work, as we see, had a wide appeal.

Amazingly, the deadline was met, and on 17 March, St Patrick's Day, 1968, a little group gathered to celebrate the installation of the seat on the towpath below Baggot Street Bridge.* Abbey Theatre actors read from the poet's works and, according to Ryan, there was not a dry eye among the lot of them. No fewer than three priests were in attendance—this was long before the revelations of appalling clerical child abuse that would drive the holy men into hiding, or at least into mufti—and the seat was duly given the blessing of the Lord, who did as he was bade and preserved it safely through the years, for it is still there today, nicely weathered and as accommodating as ever. As John Ryan prettily put it,

> In the fullness of summer, when the poplars and beeches crowd the heavens with turbulent foliage, the skies, the trees, and water all seem to merge in one quivering unity. From his seat, you will see the waters of the canal falling 'Niagarously' into the lock, and your vision, as you raise your head, will be led half a mile up the canal

---

* I would surely have attended the occasion, had I not been off in Berkeley, California, among the Afros, the cheesecloth and the riots.

until it meets the winking eye of Eustace Bridge. Then, the immense beauty of it all touches the heart. At such a moment one may concede that some Parnassian deity (a friend now of the poet) is presiding over the scene.

The other seat—on which, looking raffish and at the same time distinctly eerie, there lounges a life-sized bronze statue of the bespectacled poet, by the sculptor John Coll—was unveiled, if a seat can be said to be unveiled, by President Mary Robinson in the summer of 1991. Somehow one can guess which bench Kavanagh would have preferred.

· · · · ·

'Genius,' Baudelaire observes, 'is none other than childhood formulated with precision.' I believe that the great French *décadent*, who was writing here about the equally decadent English essayist Thomas De Quincey, author of *Confessions of an English Opium-Eater*, intended the word 'genius' to be understood in this context as the 'daimon', which the ancient Greeks believed is in every man: his character, indeed his essence. If Baudelaire is correct, then in a sense childhood never ends, but exists in us not merely as a memory or complex of memories, but as an essential part of what we intrinsically are. Every artist knows the truth of this since, for the artist, childhood and the childhood conception of things, is a deep

source of what used to be called inspiration, if for no other reason than that it was as children that we first apprehended the world as *mystery*. The process of growing up is, sadly, a process of turning the mysterious into the mundane. We cease to be amazed by things — the sky, the turning of the seasons, love, other people — only because we have grown accustomed to them.

Imagine a being from an immensely distant planet wholly dissimilar to ours, who is sent here to make a comprehensive survey of Earth and its inhabitants and report back to his government, which is contemplating the possibility of a long-range hostile take-over. He makes a quick scout round — he has fabulously fast powers of observation and absorption — and is putting the finishing touches to his report, when it begins to rain: water, falling from the sky! Or someone sneezes — what sudden seizure is this? — or yawns: what does it mean, this silent scream, and why are people roundabout not amazed and appalled by the spectacle? Our alien realises on the spot that his report will have to be torn up and begun again, for this place is far, far more strange than at first he took it to be.

The child, like that alien fact-gatherer, exists in a state of constantly recurring astonishment — at every other moment he encounters something new and extraordinary — but eventually his consciousness becomes blurred. A time comes when, as we sadly say, he has seen it all. But none of us has seen it all: everything is always new, and every time is the first time. We do not grow up; all we do is grow dull.

So the septuagenarian who sits here in damp spring weather

writing this quasi-memoir is also that child who, replete with sausage, rasher and Kylemore cake, set off on that long-ago December day aboard the number 10 bus bound for the city centre, or An Lár, as the legend on the front of the bus had it. I look back and see a seven-year-old stranger who yet *is me*. But how can that possibly be, that I am that child, and that that child is me? This question preoccupied the philosopher Wittgenstein, who set it alongside other such conundrums—Is a rose red in the dark? If a lion could speak would we understand him?—that he tried and failed, fascinatingly failed, to solve.*

Can the old man be the same being as the child he once was? I have a small white jagged scar in the space between my eyebrows, the legacy of a mishap when I was four or five. One day I was running across the Faythe, the rather oddly named square—in fact it is wedge-shaped—in Wexford where I was born, and crashed into a sharp-edged wooden post that was supporting a newly planted sapling. A couple of years ago I went back to the Faythe to have a look at the old place, and was astounded to find a grove of mature trees flourishing there. I was baffled, for they looked to me as if they had been standing for centuries. 'Ah, no,' my sister gently told me, 'they're only about as old as yourself.' Aghast, I touched a finger to

---

* Wittgenstein is commemorated by a plaque in the Palm House of the Botanic Gardens in Glasnevin. In the late 1940s the philosopher lived in Dublin, where he had a good friend, Dr Maurice Drury, a consultant psychiatrist at St Patrick's Hospital. He put up at Ross's—now the Ashling—Hotel, which displays another plaque to his memory, took his lunch at Bewley's or the Members' Dining Room at the Zoo, and sometimes sat on the steps in the warmth of the Palm House to work.

the scar on my brow, thinking: *I was here, alive, when these trees were planted!*

Is the child the father of the man, as Wordsworth claims? If so, is it not a grotesque thought to entertain in old age that one was begat by the child one started out as?

And when does the past become the past?

• • • • •

O'Connell Street had its heyday in the 1950s, before it was turned into a replica of one of Las Vegas's dingier outlying neon strips. Real trees grew there then, London planes, some of them dating back to the nineteenth century, all swept away a decade ago and replaced by scrawny nondescript growths that look as if they are made of plastic. Nelson's Pillar still stood, as handsome as it was incongruous. The buses that rumbled along both sides of the street, bellowing like elephants, were painted moss-green, and had an open platform at the back where, ignoring the conductor's wearily reiterated warning, one could leap thrillingly on or off, grasping at a burnished silver pole, while the vehicle was setting off or coming to a wallowing stop. One day I witnessed an epicene young man, as camp as Christmas, step balletically off one of those buses as it was drawing to a halt. When it had stopped, the conductor, a diminutive fellow, appeared brandishing a furled umbrella. 'Hey, fairy!' he called jeeringly, after the departing dandy. 'You forgot your wand!' The young man

stopped, turned, strolled back, took the umbrella, and tapped his taunter lightly on the shoulder with the tip of it, saying, 'Turn to shit, evil dwarf!' What a source of wit the gays were in those less than gay times, and how they did make us laugh.

Grafton Street had Switzers and Brown Thomas, but these elegant emporia were the reserve of the well-heeled; we, the somewhat lower orders, had to content ourselves with Clery's in O'Connell Street. Clery's must have been one of the largest department stores in these islands, many-storeyed, with miles of counters, and was cheerfully and irremediably shabby: I recall bare floorboards, but in this I must be mistaken, for surely there would have been linoleum, at the least. The store's male staff consisted mainly of middle-aged men who came in two varieties: there were the comedians, masters of the risqué one-liners—'That elastic's made to last, missus!'—or the distracted, faintly desperate-seeming ones who had the air, I thought, of genteel jail-birds anxiously awaiting early release on good behaviour. Their female counterparts wore black—black skirts, black twin-sets, sensible black shoes—and were brisk and competent in a martyred sort of way, like an order of secular nuns.

Our first stop was the jewellery department, where each year I was bought a ten-and-sixpenny wristwatch for my birthday. These little timepieces charmed and fascinated me: their leather straps smelt of wealth, and it was claimed they had rubies built into their works—real rubies! The ones we could afford were far down at the lower end of the range, and if I was lucky they would keep time until early in the New Year, then lose the run of themselves, either lagging in seeming exhaustion, or bounding hours ahead, with a feverishly fast tick. When they expired at last, usually around mid-February, I would revert to borrowing surreptitiously my mother's elegant little Omega from a drawer in her dressing table, for it was unthinkable that I should go among my schoolmates showing a pauper's bare wrist.

When the Ceremony of the Buying of the Watch had been completed, there was a dreary hour to endure, trailing behind my mother, my aunt and my sister as they gave themselves up to the main business of the day, the purchase of what were, to me, hopelessly dull Christmas presents. The clothes-racks of a department store hold few delights for a small boy, even one with a shiny new watch to show off. True, he could ogle the mannequins in the corsetry section, and brush the back of his hand, as if by accident, along a rack of cool and excitingly brittle-feeling nylon slips. He could dream, too, of being whisked up by the Kayser Bondor lady—'Lingerie! Housecoats! Brassieres'!—and carried off, blissfully unresisting, to her boudoir. This delightful creature, portrayed on a stand-up cardboard sign, was a tall, wasp-waisted, crimson-lipped lovely, shamelessly displaying her stocking-tops, who sashayed her lascivious way through many of my boyhood fantasies, and could probably even still, when conjured up out of the throbbing past, shake a shapely leg for my benefit and provocation.*

Treats, treats and more treats. There were at least two ice-cream

---

* She can still be viewed, as richly gowned as ever and in a variety of elegantly suggestive poses, twinkling away among the farther-off galaxies of the Internet.

TIME PIECES

parlours on O'Connell Street, the Broadway and the Palm Beach—I am told the restaurant critic Paolo Tullio's family owned one of them, or perhaps both—cheap and gaudy establishments to some eyes, no doubt, but for us as colourful as California. I favoured the Palm Beach, for its glorious Knickerbocker Glories—I can still *see* the dribble of glistening crimson syrup snaking, or rather snailing, its way down the side of the glass—its Melancholy Babies, and its even more unseemly sounding Banana Splits. Oddly, I can only remember being brought there by my brother, who was a teenager when I was still in short pants. Do I imagine it or did the Palm Beach boast a jukebox, with a sort of slot machine at each table into which one inserted a coin and chose a favourite tune? My brother was a connoisseur of the more sophisticated popular singers of the time: Frank Sinatra, Doris Day, Perry Como, Nat 'King' Cole, Rosemary Clooney, the Ink Spots, Teresa Brewer . . .

Music! Music! Music!

During those long birthdays I must have eaten something besides breakfast at my Aunt Nan's flat and a late-afternoon goblet of ice cream in rain-washed O'Connell Street. Perhaps there was lunch—we would have called it dinner—at Wynns Hotel on Abbey Street, haunt of loud whiskey-drinking priests and shady-looking types in trilbies, as well as the odd hopeful but no-longer-young lady in seamed stockings and a florid blouse, perched at the bar with a gin and tonic before her, and a cigarette, incarnadined at its lip end, clipped at a pert angle between the ostentatiously ringless fingers of her left hand.

In the dining room, under a ceiling stained honeysuckle-yellow by tobacco smoke, 'dinner' would have been a bowl of beige soup, followed by a big off-white plate on to which had been slung two or three thick slabs of grey-brown beef, accompanied by formerly green vegetables boiled to within an inch of their lives, then something with custard on it, the whole thing rounded off—or 'driven home', as George Orwell would say—with more cups of tea the colour of tree trunks sunk for centuries in swamp-water.

December days in the approach to Christmas are short, and end with a sense of soft collapse. I loved the melancholy of those Dublin evenings, despite the weight they laid upon my young heart. Railway stations at night are always incurably sad, and as the train pulled out of Westland Row at the start of the return trip to Wexford, I would have to turn my face away and press it up close against the window to hide my tears from my mother and my sister. What I saw reflected in the glass now was no dashing spy-on-the-run, but only a blubbering little boy with a heart swollen by grief. I could not have said why or for what exactly it was that I was weeping, quietly, agonisingly, with fists clenched and mouth clamped shut to prevent a sob escaping, but thinking back now, I suppose it was because something was ending, was being folded up, like a circus tent; was becoming, in short, the past.

2

Cicero, Vico and the Abbey

MY FRIEND CICERO knows a Dublin that few others are aware of or have forgotten ever existed. Over a lifetime of developing, building and collecting he has amassed a great store of arcane knowledge of a hidden city—hidden, that is, in plain view. He can tell you the pub to go to in the North Strand where on the wall of the lounge bar you will find a chart of all the lighthouses and lightships in Dublin Bay, along with their signalling sequences. He can tell you where chunks of the demolished Nelson's Pillar are to be found, and the whereabouts of the head of the admiral himself. He will show you, if you ask him nicely, the sadly dilapidated remains of what he insists is, or was, the most beautiful of the city's surviving Georgian houses, which in the aftermath of its days of glory accommodated, if that's the word, dozens of families of the poor, all jumbled together in unimaginable misery in its unsulliably handsome, high-ceilinged rooms. He is one of the prime movers in the redevelopment of Dublin's docklands, a creator of music venues and theatres, a man of taste and subtle discernment and, when it comes to the spotting of genuine antiquities, a vernacular genius.[*] In the Gravediggers pub they tip their caps to him. He knows who Blood Stoney was, and why Misery Hill is called Misery Hill. How fortunate I am to have him for a friend and, now, as my guide to the hidden city.

· · · · ·

It is a May morning of luminous loveliness. The sunlight glows through a delicate muslin mist, the soft air is fragrant with the smell of lilac, and out over the tawny reaches of Sandymount strand, where Stephen Dedalus once trod upon seaspawn and seawrack while seeking myopically to make out the signatures of all the things he was sent there to read, the pale sky shines and shimmers like the

---

[*] For the record, he founded the Point Village, 3Arena and the Bord Gáis Energy Theatre, and co-founded the National Conference Centre, the Vicar Street venue and the Gibson Hotel. A record not to be sniffed at . . . as if anyone would dare.

inner skin of a vast soap bubble. Cicero and I, a pair of devil-may-care old dogs, are motoring southwards in his little red roadster,* on the way to view the disassembled but carefully preserved frontage and side wall of the original Abbey Theatre.

The Abbey was founded by the poet W. B. Yeats and his friend Augusta, Lady Gregory, with the support of the ineffable Edward Martyn—memorably characterised by Yeats's biographer Roy Foster as 'moon-faced, obese, epicene, frantically Catholic'—of Tillyra Castle in County Galway. Financial support for the establishment of the theatre came from Miss Annie Horniman, a wealthy American who was an admirer of Yeats and a fellow dabbler in the occult. She it was who put up the money to purchase the Mechanics' Institution, on the corner of Abbey Street and Marlborough Street in the centre of Dublin. In previous lives the building had been at one time a playhouse—the Prince's—and at another a savings bank. The property also once housed the City Morgue, which fact proved a source of rich material for Dublin's mordant and unfailingly spiteful wits.

Of whom Oliver St John Gogarty was one of the sharpest and most malignant. Delighted by Miss Horniman's name, he enshrined it in a clever and scurrilous limerick:

> *What a pity it is that Miss Horniman*
> *When she wants to secure or suborn a man*

---

* It is an MG two-seater, 1,275cc, vintage 1957, 'the last of the true British sports cars', says Cicero, who bought it forty years ago, 'for a hard-earned £400'. 'Listen to the roar of that engine—it's like piloting a Spitfire.'

Should choose Willie Yeats
Who still masturbates
And at any rate isn't a horny man.

Before the establishment of the Abbey there had been the Irish National Dramatic Society, run by Frank and Willie Fay—whose legacy Yeats and Lady Gregory ignored, an instance of aristocratic disdain that the hard-working brothers bitterly resented. Despite his patrician instincts, however, Yeats had the ambition to involve the lower orders* in the new theatre. He wrote: "'Let us go to the clerks and the shop girls," one of us [most likely himself] said, "and train them for the stage after their work hours. Let us try." We found the task far easier than we expected. It was only another evidence of the spirit of intellectual interest which pervaded all classes.' This was to ignore the fact that the brothers Fay had already gathered around them and trained a talented group of amateur actors, on whose services Yeats could call, and did. In the 1890s Willie Fay's troupe had toured throughout the United Kingdom, while his brother was keenly involved in amateur dramatics in Dublin— it was the Fays who, in 1902, had put on the first production of Yeats's *Cathleen Ní Houlihan*, with Yeats's muse Maud Gonne in the leading role; the production, which played mainly to working-class audiences, was an unexpected success. What can they have made,

---

* I wonder what is the origin of this disparaging term for what used to be called 'the lower orders'. No doubt a real, true-born Dubliner could tell me. I shall ask Cicero . . .

the gurrier* groundlings, of Yeats's exalted transports as intoned by the egregious Maud?

The Abbey Theatre opened on 27 December 1904—just six months after James Joyce's momentous first date on 16 June with his future wife Nora Barnacle, of whom his father, on hearing her surname, wryly observed to his son, 'Well, she'll never leave you'—with productions of Yeats's *On Baile's Strand* and *Cathleen Ní Houlihan*, and Gregory's *Spreading the News*, playing to a full house. The evening was a triumph, especially for Yeats. Lady Gregory had come down with a dose of flu and was safely quarantined at her home, Coole Park, near Gort in County Galway, so the poet was free to bask alone in the spotlight. And there was no greater lover of that caressing glow than Willie Yeats. As Roy Foster writes, 'WBY saw himself as a dictator in the cause of art, ready to dominate, divide and rule.' Others, however, including the still smarting Fays,

> in later years would try vainly to stress that the theatrical movement which entered its apotheosis in the newly opened Abbey . . . was the product of more than one man's genius. But as far as posterity was concerned, they were irretrievably swept aside into subordinate roles by WBY's increasingly powerful sense of his own history.*

The theatre looked smaller on the outside than it actually was. It had two outer walls, a façade on Abbey Street and a flanking wall on Marlborough Street. Certain key facilities were lacking, however, including access to the stage from the dressing rooms, so that the actors, in full costume, had to race round from a side door on Marlborough Street and enter the theatre through the foyer. So, at least, legend has it . . .

· · · · ·

Killiney Bay, to the south of Dublin city, has been compared, for grandeur and beauty, with the Bay of Naples, and rightly so. The affinity is celebrated in local place names. There is Sorrento Terrace—a row of handsome houses standing at the north end of the bay—Nerano Road and Torca Road, called after towns on the Amalfi coast. George Bernard Shaw lived in Torca Cottage between 1866 and 1874. And then there is the delightful Vico Road, recalling the Neapolitan philosopher Giambattista Vico, much admired by James Joyce, who cunningly commemorated that savant in the opening lines of *Finnegans Wake*, '. . . a commodious vicus of recirculation . . .'

It is along the Vico Road that Cicero and I are headed, following

---

* Yet we might seek to temper Foster's somewhat stern judgement by recalling, in a poem such as 'The Circus Animals' Desertion', the elderly Yeats's rueful backward glances at those days when

Players and painted stage took all my love,
And not those things that they were emblems of

and he realised the hollowness of some parts at least of his achievement:

Vain gaiety, vain battle, vain repose,
Themes of the embittered heart . . .

its steeply meandering climb up the side of Killiney Hill to the home of Joan Hanly, widow of Daithí Hanly, former Dublin city architect, who died in 2003 at the age of eighty-six.

Hanly was one of the few truly enlightened public figures of his time. From the beginning of his career in the early 1940s he sought to encourage the preservation of the texture and spirit of Dublin's architectural heritage. In the 1960s he was particularly critical of so-called 'developments' such as the construction of the Electricity Supply Board's offices in Fitzwilliam Street, which required the destruction of a goodly part of a terrace of Georgian houses—'modest in themselves', in the opinion of Maurice Craig, in his captivating *Dublin 1660-1860*, first published in 1952, but 'an important part of the then intact streetscape'—and the erection at the foot of the admittedly unlovely Eden Quay of the truly hideous Liberty Hall, a truncated steel and glass tower topped with a crinkled metal flange resembling a giant waffle. He also opposed the erection of the concrete cube that is the Central Bank headquarters, squatting grossly on a graceless site halfway up Dame Street, and round which, in all seasons, even on the palmiest days of summer—and we do get the odd, very odd, palmy day in Dublin—there blows a mysterious and unabating gale.

The Abbey Theatre was destroyed by fire in 1951, and the company moved to the old Queen's Theatre in Pearse Street. In 1961 the Abbey Street building was demolished. Hanly took it upon himself to salvage the granite blocks of the front and side walls, and stored them, each fragment carefully numbered, in the grounds of his house on the Vico Road. He intended that they would be reassembled as the frontage to a national theatre museum, but his hopes in that direction came to nothing. Later, when the new Abbey Theatre was being put up on the original site at the corner of Abbey Street, he suggested that the granite façade should be incorporated into the lobby of the new building; once again he was ignored.

Hanly's tenacity in the face of official indifference and obscurantism is admirable, and so is the devotion of his widow, Joan, who persists in preserving the numbered blocks, which line the pathways of her handsome garden and turn it into a latter-day, miniature Pompeii. Cicero and I, conducted by Joan Hanly and her daughter Helen, make a tour of the site; we are touched by the melancholy of the fallen stones but enchanted by the beauty of the hillside garden and the Amalfitan view out over the vast bowl of Killiney Bay.

In a shed in a corner of the garden are preserved the theatre's windows, complete with their original glass, and, most poignant of all, the little ticket kiosk of the Peacock, the small experimental theatre established in the 1920s on the ground floor of the main theatre. And on a table there is a beautifully crafted wooden scale model of the theatre, accurate in every detail.

Standing in Joan Hanly's delightful garden, I ask myself what will happen to these tenaciously preserved remnants of a lost past, this part of a yesteryear still here today. But Cicero, it turns out, has a plan, which he promises to tell me about, some day . . .

3

Baggotonia

IT IS NOT CERTAIN—which is to say, I don't know—who it was that came up with the name. He or she was obviously thinking of Fitzrovia, London's supposedly artistic quarter that lies north of Soho. As Charlotte Street and Fitzroy Square are at the heart of Fitzrovia, so Baggot* Street and Merrion Square form the nucleus of Baggotonia. The street is called after Sir Thomas Bagod (died *c*. 1298), the first Irish chief justice, who built Baggotrath Castle, said to be the strongest fortress in the Ireland of its day. The castle subsequently passed into the ownership of the Fitzwilliam family, and later fell into ruin, although the remains of it were still

---

* On at least one eighteenth-century map the spelling is given as 'Baggat'.

standing in the early nineteenth century. It is commemorated in Baggotrath Place, which runs from Fitzwilliam Lane to Baggot Street Upper, where there used to be, and perhaps still is, the best flower stall in Dublin.

The boundaries of Baggotonia are mysteriously fluid. For the purposes of brevity, I shall here follow Nancy Mitford's example and employ the designations 'B' and 'Non-B' in referring to those things that are authentically Baggotonian and those that are not. Thus both ends of Lower Mount Street are B, but the street itself is decidedly Non-B, and wasn't even when I was young and many of its Georgian houses were still standing. At the eastern end of the thoroughfare are the canal and the leafier lower stretch of Percy Place, while at its western end it runs into Merrion Square; both these extremes are triumphantly B — are, indeed, characteristic examples of Baggotonia Superba. So what is it about the street itself that is Non-B? Even aboriginal sons and daughters of Baggotonia, of whom few, if indeed any, survive, could not tell you that; one just *knows*.

Here is another instance of the mystery, pointed out to me by Cicero: just past the junction of lowly Lower Mount Street and lordly Merrion Square is Holles Street, which runs down by the side of Holles Street maternity hospital, opposite which on many a misty morning long ago I used to huddle in hungover misery awaiting the number 7 bus. Now, Holles Street, which is quite short, is B at the top, but terrifically Non-B at the bottom, where it crosses Grand Canal Street Lower and enters the underworld of Erne Street Upper, the latter a region no self-respecting Baggotonian would venture into, except perhaps in search of bathroom fittings, or to have a new car exhaust fitted.

And then there is Harcourt Street, a gently curving Georgian stretch as handsome and as well-preserved as Upper Mount Street or Baggot Street itself. But is it B? Not quite, or at least not *quite* quite. Yet Harcourt Terrace, which lies far further beyond the B boundaries even than its Harcourt Street cousin, is an honorary B zone, if only for the reason that two of the more exotic specimens of Dublin fauna in the mid-twentieth century, the actor—the *acctorr*—Micheál Mac Liammóir and his partner, the theatrical impresario Hilton Edwards, famously lived there.

Such are the enigmas of the urban life, a life as primitive and intricately ritualised in its way as that which flourishes on the Trobriand Islands or shivers on the Arctic's tundra wastes.

· · · · ·

Speaking of Mac Liammóir and Edwards: they were the most prominent, not to say the most flagrant, representatives of the homosexual life of Dublin in those days. At the time 'queers' were the subject of much contemptuous mockery and endless smutty jokes, behind which there lurked, as there always does, a certain unease, even a certain fear. Yet Dublin, in its peculiar way, was far more tolerant of homosexuals, or at least of some homosexuals, than London or even New York, and Edwards and Mac Liammóir were regarded, indeed were cherished, as Dublin 'characters'. They ran the Gate Theatre—Orson Welles began his acting career there at the age of sixteen—with panache and what one might call careful daring, and in doing so added much glamour and richness to the admittedly sparse cultural life of the city. When Mac Liammóir died in 1978, Taoiseach Jack Lynch was among the thronging attendance at the funeral, and afterwards made a point of offering his condolences to Edwards and shaking his hand, as he would have done with any bereaved husband or wife.

Mac Liammóir, who never appeared in public without make-up and a black wig that glistened like wet coal, pretended all his life to be Irish—he spoke and wrote in the Irish language with fluency and style—but in fact he had been born Alfred Willmore in Kensal Green in London, and had not a drop of Irish blood in his veins. Besides his acting and writing in Ireland, he also had an international career, mainly in film. He played Iago in Orson Welles's movie version of *Othello*, had a role in John Huston's *The Kremlin Letter*, and was the lip-smackingly lubricious narrator of Tony Richardson's *Tom Jones*. As I once wrote of him, if he was a ham, then so were Laurence Olivier, Richard Burton and Peter O'Toole.

My favourite anecdote of Mac Liammóir was told to me by a journalist colleague from the old days, Seamus McGonagle, who himself did not lack for colour or wit. As a cub reporter Seamus was commissioned to interview the actor. Arriving at the celebrated house in Harcourt Terrace, he was treated to one of Mac Liammóir's

more dramatic entrances, as he came flouncing down the staircase in silk pyjamas and Chinese dressing gown and slippers of crimson velvet. He greeted Seamus warmly, and they repaired—with Mac Liammóir one never merely *went*—to the drawing room, where tea was served, and the great man set out, with the ponderous grace of a Cunard liner, on an account of his life and career. While he spoke, the house cat appeared and jumped on to Seamus's lap and began to claw at his flies, as cats will do. Mac Liammóir paid no attention to the creature, until its scratching, and my poor pal's embarrassment, became too intense to ignore, at which point he broke off from his oration for long enough to say to Seamus, 'Oh, don't mind him, dear boy—he's fixed.'"

· · · · ·

It was in the early 1960s that I forsook the town of my birth and moved to Dublin. And 'forsook' is the appropriate word. During the first eighteen years of my life that I spent in Wexford, I treated the place as no more than a staging post on my way elsewhere. I had so little interest in the town that I did not even bother to learn the names of most of the streets. In imaginative terms, this

---

* *The Boys*, a joint biography by Christopher Fitz-Simon, is a wonderful tribute, by turns warm and waspish, to this unique pair, while Mac Liammóir's memoir *All for Hecuba* is greatly entertaining if not always entirely reliable in matters of fact . . .

indifference to my birthplace, to its history, and to the complex and subtle life of its people, was not only arrogant but foolish, and wasteful, too. That in my immediate surroundings there was a world interesting enough to be worthy of an artist's attention—and from earliest days I had no doubt that I was going to be an artist of some kind or other—is amply attested to in the work of such Wexford writers as Colm Tóibín, Eoin Colfer and Billy Roche, all three of whom, and Roche in particular, have made a trove of rich coinage out of what I regarded as base metal, when I deigned to regard it at all.

I might defend myself, indeed I might even deny the need for such a defence, by saying that I have never in my life paid much attention to my surroundings wherever it was I happened to find myself—*artistic* attention, that is. For good or ill, as a writer I am and always have been most concerned not with what people do— that, as Joyce might say, with typical Joycean disdain, can be left to the journalists—but with what they *are*. Art is a constant effort to strike past the mere daily doings of humankind in order to arrive at, or at least to approach as closely as possible to, the essence of what it is, simply, to be. It's as legitimate for the artist to address the question of being as it is for the philosopher—as Heidegger himself acknowledged when he remarked that in his philosophising he was seeking only to achieve what Rilke had already done in poetry. No doubt he was thinking of lines such as these, from the ninth of Rilke's *Duino Elegies*—in the somewhat antiquated but sympathetic Leishman/Spender translation—which sets out by asking why we should bother to be human and live at all, then ventures this magnificent reply:

> . . . *because being here is much, and because all this*
> *that's here, so fleeting, seems to require us and strangely*
> *concerns us. Us the most fleeting of all. Just once,*
> *everything, only for once. Once and no more. And we, too,*
> *once. And never again. But this*
> *having been once, though only once,*
> *having been once on earth — can it ever be cancelled?*

Yet when I look back now at all that I rejected in those early years, and ponder the unheeding and heartless manner in which I rejected it, I am pierced with what is if not sorrow then something that feels sharply like it. I left a place that I thought harsh and ungenerous, but that in reality was tender, and too engrossed in its own hopes and sorrows to bother much with me.

My parents are first and foremost among all that I put behind me. There they lie, far off among the mirages of memory, like a pair of toppled statues against whom the sands of the years have gathered in drifts, and whose features the winds of time have blurred.

I never saw my father run. As I grow older this remarkable fact strikes me with ever more keenness and force. He must have run, of course, sometimes, on some necessary occasions, but if he did, and if I witnessed him doing so, I have no recollection of it. His life, moving at an even and unruffled pace, was limited on all sides by the circumstances of his time, his class and the age he lived in. There was, really, nowhere that he needed to run to.

To glance back over one's shoulder* at the lives of one's parents in order to make comparisons with one's own life is a dizzying exercise. It startles me to realise that when my father was the age that I am now, just embarking upon my perilous seventies, he was already long retired and entering with more or less equanimity into his dotage. My mother was more resistant to the encroachment of age and its attendant enfeeblements—she was in her late fifties when, with a great deal of nerve and no little daring, she purchased her first pair of what in those days were called slacks. My father was thoroughly bemused and, I suspect, more than a little alarmed, too, by such an uncharacteristic gesture towards liberation. But, then, he had always tended to be a stick-in-the-mud, the mud of small-town life out of which my mother never ceased striving to drag him.

A couple of years ago I came across a report of a survey by the British Department of Work and Pensions—there must not have been much news in the papers that day—which found that of the people whose opinions were canvassed, women considered old age to begin at sixty, while men, the poor saps, believed it began at fifty-eight. Those figures surprised me, given the greatly increased life-

---

* Rilke again, from the eighth Elegy:

> . . . *we always,*
> *do what we may, retain the attitude*
> *of someone who's departing . . .*

span that most of us nowadays can look forward to; but I'm sure they would not have surprised my father, or even my mother.

In her more exasperated moments my mother would say of her husband that he was born old. This was unkind, and not really a fair judgement. What made him seem prematurely elderly was, I think, the narrow range of his expectations. He worked all his life at a white-collar job—though he did wear a brown shop-coat over his suit and shirt and tie—in a large garage that supplied motor parts to much of County Wexford. Ironically, he never learned to drive a car. He was a fast walker, though, and if I concentrate I can hear again the particular clickety-click rhythm of his cleated shoe-heels on the pavement outside our house.

In the morning he would walk to work, which took him some twenty minutes. At lunchtime he would walk home, take a meal, read the newspaper for a quarter of an hour, then walk back to work. Finishing at six, he would cross the road from the garage to his brother's pub to drink a pint of Guinness before setting off for home and his 'tea'. Over nearly forty years, this schedule did not vary, except in the summer months when the rest of the family moved to the seaside and my father commuted morning and evening by train. At the time I, too, accepted all this as the necessary shape and schedule of his life, but I wonder now how much he resented the daily round, and how much the monotony of it contributed to a sense in him of lost opportunities, forfeited happiness.

But perhaps I am being patronising by thinking his life monotonous. What for me would have been a killing dullness may for him have been a comfort, and may have seemed preferable to the vain strivings that tormented so many others around him, my mother included. There is a lovely poem by Philip Larkin, the bard of senescence, called 'Next, Please', which begins by lamenting our childish notions of what life surely has in store for us:

> *Always too eager for the future, we*
> *Pick up bad habits of expectancy.*

For my mother, as for me, life was always elsewhere. She, too, reminds me, as in my Wexford days I used to remind myself, of Chekhov's Irina, immured in the provinces and yearning for the magic of Moscow. Yet she, too, like my father, was forced to live to a programme. She was a housewife. Housewiving was a job—though she would never have thought of it as any such thing—that she performed diligently and well. She went 'down the town' to do the shopping every morning, except on Sundays, when no shops were open. On weekdays there was the grocer's to be called on, and the greengrocer's, the butcher's, the baker's . . . I wonder how many shopping bags she wore out in her lifetime of 'going for the messages'.

I do not have to wonder about my mother's levels of discontent, as I do about my father's. Although of necessity stoical in the face of general disappointment, she was given to outbursts of frustration and complaint. She read more widely than my father, and so I suppose she had more of an inkling of what the world of elsewhere had to offer, and of all that she was missing.

She was a devotee of *Woman* and *Woman's Own*. I have no idea what these magazines are like nowadays—I hope they have not given in to the universal obsession with the imaginary lives and dubious loves of soap-opera characters—but at that stage of their existence they concerned themselves mostly with the Royal Family, with knitting patterns, and with recipes for such delights as steak-and-kidney pie and, that ultra-smart staple of the day, prawn cocktail. They were wholly innocent publications, although my sister is adamant that one April Fools' Day one or other of them ran an article headed: 'Knit Yourself a Lovely Dutch Cap'. My mother, I have no doubt, would not have got the joke. Indeed, perhaps no one under my own age would get it now, either.

These two magazines, largely identical in content and tone, were for my mother a splash of colour in a drab time. Then one day in the confessional, being short, I suppose, of peccadilloes to own up to, she mentioned to the priest that she read them—he had probably been probing to know if she was keen on what he would have called 'dirty books'—and he promptly ordered her to stop buying them, under pain of mortal sin. I was fifteen or so at the time, and argued with her that the priest was a fool and had no idea what *Woman* and *Woman's Own* were like and probably thought them sister publications of such scandal sheets as *Titbits* or, dear Lord, the *News of the World*. My argument had no effect. My mother, obedient daughter of the Church that she was, cancelled her subscription to both mags, and so ceased to keep up with the state of health of the Queen's corgis or the latest thing in Christmas-cake decoration.

My mother must have been in her forties at that time. Can one imagine now a middle-aged woman succumbing to such an absurd and petty commandment, even in Ireland, where even still, among many Catholics, the Church despite all its efforts has not succeeded in discrediting itself entirely? The world of fifty years ago was a very different place from ours.

In my ruminations on the pedestrian pace of my father's life, it occurred to me to calculate that in the past few years I have made trips to America, North and South, and, in Europe, to Spain, France, Germany, Italy, Portugal and Greece, as well as Poland and Estonia—there are bound to have been a few other destinations that have slipped my mind—clocking up who knows how many thousands of air miles and, as a consequence, suffering successive onslaughts of jet lag. Such travels would have been beyond not only my father's but even my mother's imaginings, and she would be incredulous and bitterly condemnatory of my jadedness and lack of excitement at the prospect of making more journeys in the coming year to other far-flung elsewheres.

When I was young myself I did not think of my parents as being either young or old. To me they seemed, until their final years, to be of an indeterminate age, creatures essentially of a different species, permanent and unchanging, simply *there*. I do not remember registering signs of their ageing, even when I had moved to Dublin and made increasingly infrequent visits 'home'. They were, in my view of them, stranded in a timeless zone, preserved in the permafrost of what had already begun to be, for me, the past. Did my mother, like the women in that British survey, think of herself as old when she reached sixty? Did my father hear the distant, dark tolling of a funeral bell when he passed fifty-eight?

I wonder now increasingly what they made of me. As a little boy I was, I think, not unpleasant—my mother, at any rate, doted on me—but in my teenage years I suspect I must have been wholly obnoxious: selfish, discontent, at once detached and demanding, and of a lordly arrogance based on nothing more than my own overblown estimation of what I would one day achieve. Such a trial I must have been, especially to my mother, who, throughout my childhood and adolescence, saw so much more of me, and put up with much more from me, than my father did.

I left home with a cruel insouciance, shaking the dust of Wexford from my heels and heading for what I took to be the dazzlingly bright lights of Dublin. It must have been a wrench for my parents to see me go, so carelessly and with hardly a backward glance. I was the last of their children, and now the household that once had numbered five was reduced to its original two. How lonely my mother must have felt in the middle of weekday afternoons without the prospect of my coming in from school, no matter how surly and uncommunicative a presence I may have been. I imagine her watching the winter darkness approaching across the fields that faced our house and knowing in her heart that she would never now get to see the places of her dreams. She did move to Dublin, she and my father, late in their lives, where they shared a house with my accommodating and endlessly forbearing brother. But it was, by then, too late, I think: Dublin was not Moscow, was not, indeed, the Dublin she had dreamed of, since that Dublin was just that—a dream.

Both my parents were dead before I was thirty-five. I mourned them, of course, but how much of my mourning was for them, and how much of it was in reality a first inkling of my own suddenly all too plausible mortality? In their going they were as considerate and as diffident as they had been in life. My mother fell down dead of a heart attack while feeding the birds in her garden one gloriously golden afternoon in September; a few years later my father faded away quietly in a nursing home. When I heard of his death I remember thinking suddenly: *Now I am an orphan*. By then I was married with children of my own, and the notion of having been orphaned, although faintly ridiculous, was compelling, too. Something, which I am not so hard-hearted as to call a burden, something had fallen away, like a cliff into the sea, and I was the lighter for it.

My youngest daughter, who is nineteen and a last child, as I was, drinks endless cups of tea, just as my mother did. Also, she prefers to walk to wherever she is going, rather than taking a lift or travelling on the bus. One day recently I watched her setting off into the morning's milky light and thought there was something familiar about her gait— she walks rapidly, favouring her left side and turning her left foot outwards a little at each step. Who was it, I wondered, that walked like that? It was only when I turned aside and caught the quick, syncopated rhythm of her heels on the pavement that I suddenly heard in memory my father's footsteps. It is in the forms of the living that the dead most convincingly haunt us.

· · · · ·

In Dublin I settled straight away into the heart of Baggotonia. By that time my Aunt Nan had moved from her grim cramped quarters in Percy Place to the shabby splendours of a flat in Upper Mount Street, which she shared successively with my sister, and later with me. The flat occupied the entire second floor of a four-storeyed Georgian terrace house, and consisted of two enormous rooms with lofty ceilings, high sash windows and eighteenth-century wooden floors so perilously worn that they thrummed like trampolines under the lightest tread.

The front room of the flat had been sectioned off to allow for the installation of a makeshift kitchen, thus destroying the room's original gracious proportions; it always gave me a grim little shock to glance up and see the carved plaster moulding under the ceiling halt suddenly when it came smack up against the partition wall. The back room, my bedroom, had been left untouched—since the eighteenth century, it seemed—and was so enormous that it was impossible to heat: there was many a winter morning when I woke up to find ice on the *inside* of the eight-foot-tall window beside my bed.

The flat had two entry doors, the main one, and another that led from my bedroom directly on to the landing. This meant that when I

was leaving in the morning or coming back at night I did not have to go through the front living room, where my aunt had her bed, which by day was turned into a sofa so lumpy that, in after years, no girl I brought to the flat would consent to sit, much less recline, upon it. In the living room there was a large circular dining table, on the surface of which the original French polish had degenerated into a sort of viscous blackish gum, and four rickety bentwood chairs that would cry out in panic-stricken protest when sat upon. A sideboard the size of a hippopotamus took up an entire wall opposite the window; it had a top of funereal greyish marble, and was backed by a wood-framed, belle-époque looking-glass in the dim and stippled depths of which my reflection would loom with a curiously malignant, Jack the Ripperish aspect.

I wonder what we burned in the fireplace in the living room. Coal or turf, certainly, or both—but where did we store the fuel, and, more puzzling still, how did we get rid of the ash? So many details fall out of the memory, like the pennies that spilled from the pockets of my trousers when I slung them over the back of the chair beside my bed at the end of yet another youthful drink-befuddled evening. I have never understood the attractions of the *vie de bohème*. Squalor is squalor, in whatever *époque*, and at whatever age one is, young or old. When in my Benjamin Black crime novels I gave that Mount Street flat to my protagonist Quirke, I smartened it up considerably.

In spring and autumn we let the hearth lie idle, and made do with a single-barred electric fire. Do people use electric fires nowadays?— are they even manufactured any more? The thing had the look, to my fanciful eye, of one of those garish fly-catching plants that squat in jungle clearings with a glowing red tongue enticingly exposed. It made good toast, though, I remember that. I remember, too, the extensible metal toasting fork on which we impaled the slices of bread, an ancient implement of uncertain provenance, black and polished by use.

Strange: I recall so many trivial things, and forget so very many momentous ones.

Our neighbours on the ground floor were an elderly, secretive couple, he a short wiry fellow with a bristling moustache that Hitler would not have scorned, and she a timid creature who wore flowered frocks in all seasons and, unless my memory is playing another of its tricks on me, a bejewelled gilt headdress, somewhat in the manner of a tiara, encrusted with rhinestones. If on entering the house one were to forget to shut the front door with anything more than feathery quietness, her husband would pop out terrier-like to complain of the noise, which, he claimed, was a grave disturbance to 'the missus'. This was curious, as he also claimed that the missus was 'as deaf as a post'. I don't know if that was true or just one of his fancies—I suspect he was a little mad—since in all the years I lived there the poor woman never spoke a word to me, or gave me cause to speak a word to her.

The top floor of the house, the one above ours, that is, was overrun—it is the only word for it—by a family of provincial folk, farming stock, to judge by their accents and demeanour. How or why they had come to live in the city was another of the mysteries of that mysterious house. It was impossible to calculate how many people were up there, as the numbers varied from week to week; I suspect the flat was a sort of miniature Ellis Island, the first landing-stage for immigrants moving from the country to settle in the city. The 'flight from the land' was fully airborne in those years, as more and more young people abandoned the farms their families had worked for generations and moved to the city, made restless by the dawning Age of Aquarius, so-called, and drawn urbanwards by the allure of television advertising—RTÉ television began broadcasting on New Year's Eve 1961. A few years later a famously reactionary and, not incidentally, anti-Semitic politician, Oliver J. Flanagan, proclaimed in Parliament that there had been no sex in Ireland before the coming of television. One sort of saw what he meant, though most of us, and especially young males such as myself, were still impatiently awaiting the arrival of the promiscuity Mr Flanagan seemed to see flourishing in flagrant abundance all round him.*

The head of the top-floor brood was a spare, spry old fellow, either an elderly father or a young grandfather, I never discovered which, who used to sit on the stairway of an evening quietly playing jigs and reels and sweetly mournful slow airs on his fiddle. He was

---

* It is worth noting that Flanagan used his maiden speech in the Dáil in July 1943 to denounce the Jews, 'who crucified Our Saviour nineteen hundred years ago, and now are crucifying us every day in the week . . . There is one thing that Germany did, and that was to rout the Jews out of their country. Until we rout the Jews out of this country it does not matter a hair's breadth what orders you make [he was speaking about the wartime Emergency Powers Acts]. Where the bees are there is the honey, and where the Jews are there is the money.' In the general election the following year he doubled his vote; in 1978 he was created a Knight of the Order of St Gregory the Great by Pope John Paul I.

affable and gentle, and obviously pined for his lost or abandoned 'home place'. He had a careworn young wife—either that or she was his daughter—and there were some sons, or cousins, enormous saturnine fellows who would shoulder past me on the stairway with rough shyness. Most memorable, however, was a girl, in her mid-teens, a creature of unreally ethereal beauty, blonde-haired, blue-eyed and tawny of limb—to whom saucy young Miss Reck of Percy Place could not have held a match, much less a candle—a voluptuous and only slightly superannuated Lolita, displaying that sulky, surly manner which Nabokov numbered among the first prerequisites of the true nymphet. How such a breathtakingly lovely creature had sprung to being in that family of perfectly decent but decidedly unlovely country folk I do not know—but, then, my dentist assures me that a certain conformation of my gums is incontrovertible evidence that I have Inca blood in my veins. Inca blood!

I believe that for a time she had, this post-Lolita, a crush on me—I would find my name scrawled in crayon on the inside of the front door, accompanied by an arrowed heart—and who knows what would have developed between us had she been a few years older? Later on she was to become a successful fashion model, and I would see her photograph from time to time in the newspapers or on the covers of the one or two semi-glossy magazines the country could boast at the time; as a grown-up she was beautiful still, but to my regretful eye an essential aspect of her beauty had evaporated along with the dew of her youth.

She had a constant sidekick, a jolly plump little person who would wheeze with suppressed laughter every time she laid eyes on me. One day some years later I wandered into Parsons bookshop on Baggot Street Bridge and there she was, older but still well-fleshed, and serving behind the counter; I could see by the look in her eye that she still thought I was a scream.

But wait. As I think back now, the possibility suddenly occurs: was it in fact Lovely from Upstairs who had the crush on me, or the Roly-poly Pal? At this distance, it hardly matters, I know, but still . . .

The most illustrious tenant of the Mount Street house — the 'Upper' will be silent from here on, except when specificity is demanded — was Anne Yeats, the daughter of W. B. Yeats. She occupied the flat on the floor below ours. She was a large shy short-sighted person in her middle years, a fine if unadventurous painter with a middling reputation that unfortunately has not endured. She was friendly and unassuming, and she and I would stop on the stairs occasionally to chat about the weather, or the deplorable state of the plumbing in the house, or the Jehovah's Witness who called upon us weekly with unrebuffable fervour and persistence — he wore a belted raincoat and a trilby hat and spoke with a pronounced Cockney accent, and reminded 'Miss Yeats', as she always was to my aunt and me, of a spiv straight out of an Ealing comedy.

The oddest observable fact about Miss Yeats was that she used to take delivery every week of two ounces of fresh yeast dispatched directly from the Dublin Yeast Company in College Green. I would see the neat little brown-paper package where the postman had left it on the hall table, and wonder what possible use Miss Yeats could have for such substantial and constant quantities of the stuff. She did not make bread with it—we would have smelt the loaves baking—and I could think of no use she could possibly put it to in her painting. Nor could I imagine that the daughter of William Butler Yeats, Nobel laureate and contentious member of the Irish Senate, would have been running a micro-brewery in her back bedroom. Another unsolved riddle from the annals of number thirty-something Upper Mount Street.

One afternoon I encountered Miss Yeats outside the door of her flat in the company of a little old woman wearing a woollen hat resembling an upside-down flowerpot, a heavy overcoat and large spectacles. I passed by with a murmured greeting, and the old lady turned and looked at me—merely looked, calmly, unenquiringly, and without uttering a word. I had the impression of eyes so dark as to be almost black, and with a peculiar intensity behind them that this chance encounter on a stairway with a callow young man should hardly have warranted. Many decades later I was commissioned to review Ann Saddlemyer's fine biography, *Becoming George: The Life of Mrs W. B. Yeats*, and flicking through the photographs in the volume, I was instantly transported back to that afternoon outside the door of Miss Yeats's flat, and realised, with a strange, vibrating shock, who the woman was who had turned and given me the look that should have been blank but had not been blank at all.

Georgie Yeats, 'Mrs W. B.', as everyone called her in the long years of her widowhood, was well-known as a dispenser of hospitality, advice and encouragement to the generation of Dublin writers that

flourished, if that is the word, just before mine arrived and tried to elbow them out of our way. As I stared at the photographs of Mrs W. B. in Professor Saddlemyer's book, what struck me most forcibly, and made me shiver, was the vividness with which I remembered, how I *saw again*, the look the old lady had given me on the landing that day all those years before. I had always been sceptical of Georgie Yeats's 'automatic writing', in which her husband encouraged her and which he set great store by, but merely to have lived within the ambit of that extraordinary gaze—some said her eyes were blue, others, and I am with them, insisted they were black—would have been inspiration enough for any poet, even one as great as Yeats. I still feel a chill ripple along my spine when I recall chancing on those photographs and being shot through again by such a penetrating glance, straight out of the past.

· · · · ·

For two years I lived in sometimes companionable but more often uneasy cohabitation with my aunt, until, with awful abruptness, she died. She had suffered from angina pectoris for many years, and one evening, sitting on a couch at the home of a kindly Jewish couple, whose children she sometimes looked after, she expired so quietly and with so little fuss that the children playing at her feet didn't notice she was gone, until their father came in and found her reclining there lifeless and, I hope, at peace at last.

I was away in the isles of Greece at the time, and my family, considerate people that they are, tried to contact me on Mykonos, but failed, so that I arrived home, suntanned and with the salt of the Aegean still in my hair—what long locks we cultivated in those hirsute times!—to receive the bad news with a kind of absent-minded incredulity. She had been so much alive, how could she be so suddenly dead? I call to mind now her irreverence, her grim brand of gaiety, her wild laughter, her disdain of the falsely pious and humourless boobies set to lord it over us. I recall the lamb chops she used lovingly to cook for me. I recall the fur bootees she favoured, winter and summer. I recall the fact that she knew Audrey Hepburn's father, who lived in Fitzwilliam Square, and who had been, I am sure she would have been surprised to learn, a keen supporter of the Nazis. I recall the evenings, all too rare, when she and I sat together in front of the one-barred electric fire, toasting bread and talking about . . . about what? Gone, all gone. On that night, when I came from the airport to my sister's house and heard our Aunt Nan was dead, I was young and heartless, and the liberation of spirit I had found in Greece was more real to me than the death of an ageing relative.

Forgive me, dear old aunt; forgive the young beast that I was, and that I regret to say I have never quite ceased to be—I am old now, or oldening, at least, but one's inner monster stays forever young.

• • • • •

I was spared so much. I returned to the flat in Mount Street with half my mind still on that rocky isle in the dark-indigo Aegean—at the time Mykonos was still an unspoiled Paradise, having not only no airport but no paved roads, either. My kindly and, where I am concerned, long-suffering sister came and cleared away Aunt Nan's things. I should have been the one to perform that painful chore; I should have been the one to suffer through such an emotionally turbulent task. But, no, I was the baby of the family, the charmed one, and must be shielded from life's more outrageous impositions.

4

On the Street

COULD NOT HAVE LIVED in a lovlier location. The view from the Natural History Museum along Merrion Square and Mount Street to St Stephen's Church—the Pepper Canister, as it is fondly called—is one of the most handsome and dignified prospects in any of the world's cities that I know or have visited. Leinster, originally Kildare, House,* which is now the seat of government, was built in the 1740s by the Earl of Kildare, James FitzGerald, in an unfavoured and marshy area south of the river

---

* Maurice Craig doubts the suggestion that the White House in Washington is a copy of Leinster House. However, the architect of the White House, James Hoban, was born in County Kilkenny, studied architecture at the Dublin Society's School 'where in 1780 he was awarded a prize for "stairs, roof &c", and in 1792 won the White House competition'.

Liffey. Poor though the site might be, the canny earl predicted that fashion would soon follow him, and he was right: before the end of the century the bulk of the city's aristocracy had moved southwards across the river. The result was that in the following century, rich redoubts such as Henrietta Street and Rutland Square would fall into decrepitude and be sold off to rack-renting landlords, so that much of the north inner city was transformed into one of the worst slums in Europe. Meanwhile, on the south side of the river there grew up around Leinster House a grid of elegant streets and boulevards, a large number of which are still intact and in use today, though most of the fine old houses have been given over to office space.

A lot of the Georgian city was still standing when I first came to live there, but a lot of it was gone, too. It is a fact, as Maurice Craig pointed out as recently as 1992, that 'much more of Dublin survives, and in reasonable order, than might be deduced from listening to the lamentations of those who deplore its destruction', but all the same, in the postwar years and up to the end of the 1960s, the city was subjected to appalling bouts of officially sanctioned destruction. The ultra-nationalist ideologues who ran the country then had scant regard for the delights of Georgian architecture, and indeed many of them would have seen Georgian Dublin as a despised monument to our British conquerors, who had been driven out in the War of Independence at the start of the 1920s.[*] Hence permissions were liberally given for large-scale despoliation of, in Yeats's words, 'many ingenious lovely things'. A particularly deplorable instance of urban mutilation was the demolition of a large stretch of the south side of

Fitzwilliam Street, to make way for the building of the Electricity Supply Board's headquarters—one of the developments that Daithí Hanly had so passionately opposed. Had the state coffers been in a more healthy state, it is likely that many other such streets would have been razed to make way for the New Brutalism. There was even a plan to fill in the Grand and Royal Canals and build super-roads over them, with sewers underneath. And the bosky green heart of delightful Merrion Square, which was then the property of the Catholic Church, barely escaped having a monster cathedral erected on it, at the behest of the unspeakable Archbishop McQuaid.[†]

In 1969, Green Property—my Mount Street landlords, as it happened—a development company with strong links to the ruling Fianna Fáil party, were given permission by the then Minister for Local Government to knock down a large chunk of Hume Street, another fine example of Georgian architecture, that leads from Ely Place on to St Stephen's Green. When the plan became public, the buildings were promptly occupied by a band of architectural students, who in time were joined by a number of public figures, including Garret FitzGerald, a Member of Parliament who would

---

[*] I remember the archaeologist Máire De Paor telling me back in the 1980s how at some public event or other she had buttonholed Charles Haughey, our then Taoiseach—who prided himself, rightly in some respects, on being a man of culture—and urged him that the state should purchase a collection of precious Georgian silver that was in danger of being lost to the country at auction. The reply she got, delivered with the famous Haugheyan snarl, was that 'The Brits are welcome to their bloody spoons.'

[†] Who, I notice, pops up repeatedly in these pages, rather like the figure of Punch in a puppet show; and in fact, when I think of it, he did bear something of a physical resemblance to that cudgel-wielding mischief-maker of the fairgrounds of old.

later become Taoiseach, and the future President of Ireland, Mary Robinson. However, late one night Green Property sent in a demolition crew, who destroyed the roofs and much of the interiors of the houses. In the end the company was compelled to erect fake Georgian buildings on the spot—'unconvincing paraphrases masquerading as replicas', in Maurice Craig's disdainful judgement—while the rest of the street was saved.

Strangely, perhaps, none of this seems to have had much effect on me. The truth is, I had little interest in Dublin's past, and not much in its present, either, if it came to that. What was it to me that in its days of glory Dublin had been the second city of the British Empire—'the finest classical city in Europe', according to the architectural historian Mark Girouard—or that it was unique in having two major canals, or that the Duke of Wellington had been born in Merrion Street opposite what is now the Department of the Taoiseach? For me, as a writer in the making, the fact was that Joyce had seized upon the city for his own literary purposes and in doing so had used it up, as surely as Kafka did with the letter K, and consequently the place was of no use to me as a backdrop for my fiction. True, some of my early short stories take place in an identifiable Dublin, but they could as well have been set in London, or Paris—or Moscow, for that matter. It was not until much later, when I invented my dark brother Benjamin Black, that I saw the potential of 1950s Dublin as a setting for his *noir* novels.

Thus in this wise I largely ignored Dublin, as I had largely ignored Wexford. Again, I seek to comfort and perhaps even exonerate myself with the thought that this is what artists do, the imagination being their only true place in which richly to live. But am I convinced? Some years ago I was asked to contribute to a collection of six-word 'stories', along the lines of Hemingway's masterpiece — one of the best things he ever wrote: 'For sale: baby shoes, never worn.' My contribution to the volume may seem facetious, but it contains a serious and bitter truth: 'Should have lived more, written less.'

Yet I was happy in those early years, after my aunt died and I took over her ninety-nine-year lease on the Mount Street flat — happier, indeed, than I realised at the time. And how I loved my particular patch of Dublin. I recognise now that for all my cosmopolitan aspirations, mine was essentially a small-town sensibility, and that Baggotonia was my ideal Wexford-sized vicinity, beyond the borders of which I ventured with reluctance. Thus I remained disgracefully ignorant of, for instance, the medieval quarters of the city, around Swift's St Patrick's Cathedral and Guinness's brewery, or, on the north side, the even older village of Howth and environs — although eventually I was to settle there, in the days when it was still a thriving fishing village; I recall taking my two young sons for walks along the west pier and seeing fishermen in wooden clogs packing kegs of salted herring for export to Britain and Scandinavia; those scenes hang in my memory, colourful and busy and antiquated, like genre pieces by one of the minor Dutch masters.

Of the suburbs I knew nothing at all, and recoiled from the prospect of all those acres of housing estates and soot-blackened factories, dotted here and there with littered patches of green where

Traveller children galloped bareback on piebald ponies, and where in my overheated imagination of such places wild-eyed young men with Brylcreemed hair engaged in gang warfare, and wives were beaten and girls were got in the family way, and at night the barn-sized pubs throbbed with a drunken din, and life in general was irredeemably squalid.

What a prissy and purblind young man I was, a snob with nothing to be snobbish about.

· · · · ·

Even in the early 1960s there were few private apartments in Mount Street, and at six o'clock in the evening, when the office workers had gone home, a vast and dreamy silence would descend upon the area. The weekends, too, were wonderfully quiet. One lemony sunlit Sunday in July, in the unpeopled hour after dawn, I was walking down Mount Street when I heard from an open garret window high above me the sounds of a woman lost in the ecstasy of love-making, her cries like a series of increasingly fast, increasingly tightening tiny needle stitches in the sharply etched air.

And speaking of love and its distraught raptures, it was in the summer months that the prostitutes came out—oh, well-named Mount Street!—to ply their busy trade. In those white nights the cruising cars would make a continuous hushed hissing, like the sound of a fast-running river, from twilight into the early hours, below my front window. It was rumoured that one of the houses in Mount Street Crescent, hard by the Pepper Canister church, was a working brothel, but I never could identify which house it might be. Anyway, most of the 'girls' prowled the streets for custom, though they must have had rooms somewhere about—perhaps in the warren of lanes and alleyways between Upper and Lower Mount Streets. I recall with special vividness two wraith-like creatures, sisters possibly, draped in scanty, crow-black dresses, who operated as a pair—for company, no doubt, and perhaps protection—and who always had a melancholy smile for me even though they knew, simply by the look of me, that I wasn't customer material. I would have liked to ask them about their lives, and how they had come to be on the streets, but I was always too timid to stop and talk to them. Could they still be in existence somewhere, married, perhaps, with grown children? Vertiginous speculation. Maybe they managed somehow to get off the game, and survive, and even thrive.

Maybe.

There was, too, a much older woman—she must have been in her fifties, fat and frumpish—who had a limp and patrolled her beat with the aid of a stout malacca cane. All the same, despite her age and lameness, she did surprisingly brisk business. One warm summer evening as I was leaving the house she accosted me at the foot of the front steps under the pretence of needing a light for her cigarette. I muttered that I had no matches, and hurried on, more frightened than repulsed. When I returned home, at midnight, she was still there, looking frustrated and peevish—it must have been a slow

night. Again she showed me her unlit cigarette and asked for a match, but when I again shouldered past her she called after me wearily, 'Ah, Jaysus, son, I really only wanted a light for me fag!' I try to call her features to mind, and see only hollow, rouged cheeks and a painted-on mouth. She, certainly, would be long gone by now. I wonder where and in what circumstances she ended her days, and I shudder.

Once and only once I did pluck up the courage, and it was Dutch courage, at that—I was on the way home from a party—to speak to one of these sad creatures of the night. And truly, as I saw, she was hardly more than a child, huddled in the darkness by the railings in Merrion Square—I might have missed her had it not been for the throbbing glow-worm that was the lighted tip of her cigarette. She was pitiably pretty, with a little moon-shaped face and a fringe that almost hid her eyes. When I stopped I could see her gathering her forces to face the business of 'doing business'. However, I quickly let her know that business was not what I was interested in. This left us both at a loss, and we stood for a moment in helpless silence, while the greenery behind the railings made its dreamy nocturnal murmurings. Then I heard myself asking her, as if I were a parent myself, whether her father knew that she was out here, like this, so late at night. At first she was surprised, but then a glitter of sour amusement came into her eye. 'Oh, yes,' she said, with a dry chuckle, 'he knows, all right.' The words were nothing, but in her tone I clearly heard the record of years of neglect, abuse and cruelty. It was too much for me, and I turned from her and skulked guiltily away into the night.

How it haunts the heart, the unfathomable mystery of other people's lives, of other people's misfortunes.

I was fascinated, on those febrile summer evenings, to sit on the old bench seat at my front window and study, for as long as daylight lasted, the trade going on down in the street. It was puzzling to see how presentable and 'ordinary' the prowling men seemed. I took most of them to be married, though please do not ask me in what way a married man might look different from a single one. If they were husbands, I suppose they were after 'something special'—like the third split of champagne that an Aer Lingus air hostess, which is what they were still called back then, pressed on me, with a wink and a lewd grin and the whispered words, 'Ah, go on, it's like a blow-job: you'll hardly ever get it at home.'

Clients came in all sorts and shapes and, as far as I could make out, from all classes, too. A story went about at the time that one night in Mount Street a prominent government minister was kerb-crawling and in his eagerness to spot a likely girl failed to notice a road works sign and let the side wheels of his Jaguar sink into a deep trench that had been dug that day by Post Office workers installing telephone lines. In a panic the grandee abandoned the car and fled. There was a cover-up, needless to say: in the middle of the night a squad of plain-clothes gardaí arrived and hauled the vehicle out of the trench and towed it discreetly away. The girls in the street were greatly amused by the incident, for the politician was a regular customer and notorious among them for his sexual voraciousness; after that night their nickname for him was 'Holy Joe' . . .

And now, suddenly, the thought of those workmen and that trench bring back to me, out of time's not-quite oblivion, the recollection of an encounter I had one morning in Mount Street with a man in a manhole—I wonder if he might have been part of that same Post Office crew whose handiwork had caused Holy Joe to come a cropper. I was crossing the street when the cover of the manhole flew open as I was about to step on it. A head in a hard hat popped up and the fellow stared at me. Without missing a beat, he put on a wild look and asked urgently, 'Is the war over?' Every trade has its comedians.

• • • • •

Diarmuid Ó Gráda's *Georgian Dublin: The Forces that Shaped the City** is an elegantly written, scrupulously researched, handsomely produced and simmeringly indignant study that concentrates as much on the squalor and misery of eighteenth-century Dublin as it does on the city's architectural and cultural splendour. It is this splendour, Ó Gráda notes, that has attracted most of the attention of previous writers on the subject. However, 'it would be incorrect,'

---

* It might seem that Ó Gráda is more alive to the social disparities of the time than Maurice Craig. However, Craig, too, has no illusions about the contrasts between the life of the aristocracy and of the populace at large in Georgian Dublin: commenting on how much of the old city was still intact when he was writing his book in the late 1940s, he writes: 'Poverty had been to a large degree the preservative, and no one can regret the economic improvement which soon afterwards began.'

he (under)states, to infer from its surviving glories

> that Dublin was amongst the best regulated European
> capitals during the second half of the eighteenth century.
> On the contrary, overcrowding and filth reached epic
> proportions in Dublin, and there were periods when the
> city was running out of control. This chaos was mainly
> due to the unrest of the anonymous.

In a harrowing chapter on prostitution, the author portrays the
scale of the ongoing catastrophe in which so many women found
themselves caught up. Girls newly up from the country, most of
them without a word of English, went into domestic service where
they were frequently abused and had no alternative but to go on the
streets. Also, men were increasingly taking over jobs formerly left
to women, such as 'hairdressing, stay-making, shoemaking and'—
even!—'midwifery as well as the teaching of music, dance, writing and
foreign languages'. An estimate of the numbers of women involved
in prostitution must remain conjectural, he writes, although

> the number of women arrested might . . . suggest the
> scale of the trade. For example, seventeen soliciting
> females were detained in a single raid on Copper Alley
> in September 1788. A few nights later watchmen rounded
> up thirty-two women around St Stephen's Green. More
> dramatically, about 150 prostitutes were apprehended in

forty-eight hours during July 1799 in the Rotunda and St Stephen's Green areas.

The financial returns, too, are telling. The pimp Margaret O'Brien quitted the city with six hundred pounds in earnings; Margaret Leeson, 'the doyenne of Dublin madams', retired in 1792 and bought a house in Blackrock for, again, six hundred pounds. 'Elizabeth McClean, one of the city's most successful madams, had a dowry of £4,000 when she got married in 1798.' These are very large sums indeed for, as Ó Gráda informs us, 'In many cases today's prices would be a hundred times greater than those of the Georgian era.'

Love, oh, careless love . . .

• • • • •

I am convinced, and will not cede in my conviction to any expert, that there is a special and unique quality to the bricks of which so much of Georgian Dublin is built. People speak of 'red-brick' houses, but red is the least of it: the colours range from rosy pink through cadmium yellow and yellow ochre to a chalky-textured madder, and burnt sienna, and patches, tiny patches, of a strangely aquatic, darkly shining purplish blue that seems to be picked out only by the light of certain late-summer evenings. The hues alter subtly with each passing hour, from an early-morning watery paleness to twilight's glowing umbrage. And when it rains, ah, when it rains the bricks gleam and

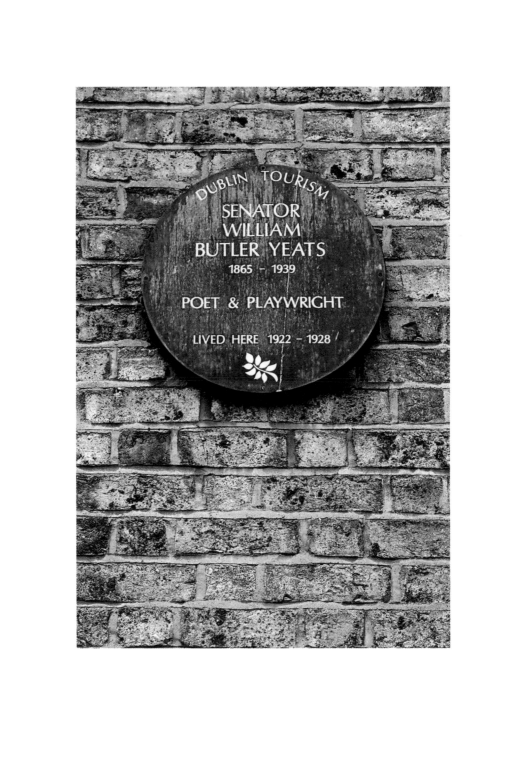

glitter like the flanks of a galloping racehorse. Even at night they exude a faint waxen glow, which somehow gives to the houses a tight-lipped, secretive aspect, as if they are pondering and digesting the day's doings in the street below, to which they were a mute and watchful witness. And the great windows, how they flare and flash, furnace-white, with the sun on them, at dawn and dusk especially, when they seem to be themselves the source of their own radiance.

The city breathes, it has its own life, apart from us, who are its parasites, its termites, its relentless, teeming virus.

· · · · ·

Much has been written, and much, much more spoken, about literary Dublin in the period from about the beginning of the Second World War—a war famously known in neutral Ireland as the Emergency—to the mid-1960s, when it all more or less came to dust with the deaths, in rapid succession, of three of the city's most notorious 'characters': Brendan Behan, Flann O'Brien and Patrick Kavanagh. Many of the younger set lived on, of course, and flourished: Thomas Kinsella, Baggotonia's poet laureate—see his lovely poem 'Baggot Street Deserta', so redolent of the period;* Brooklyn-born John

---

* *The window is wide*
  On a crawling arch of stars, and the night
  Reacts faintly to the mathematic
  Passion of a cello suite . . .

Montague, who abandoned the rough fields of his County Tyrone boyhood for Dublin's shabby splendours; the poet and critic Anthony Cronin, who in *Dead as Doornails* wrote one of the best and most shrewdly judged books about the period; the wonderful and disgracefully neglected short-story writer Mary Lavin,* who lived in Lad Lane off Upper Baggot Street; and the legendary—a tired word, but the aptest here—J. P. 'Mike' Donleavy, author of *The Ginger Man*.

The painter Francis Bacon, by the way, was born in Baggot Street, though he lost no time in departing, not only from the street but from the country, too.

No doubt I shall be shouted at for saying so, but the loudest among the legends produced precious little, although the little they did produce was precious. The hub of their raucous world was McDaids pub off Grafton Street, where many a masterpiece was talked into thin air and spirited away by the fumes of alcohol. I suppose in their heyday the McDaidians made the best of a bad time and place, and managed to have some fun, and even do a little work, into the bargain. But they lived in an undisciplined time, and they lacked living exemplars. Their heroes, or at least the mighty ones to whom they paid lip service, were gone: Yeats had died in 1939 in the South of France, Joyce in 1941 in Zürich—the latter's attitude to his native land is neatly summed up in a line from the comically

---

* Mother of my dear lost friend, the late Caroline Walsh, who succeeded me as books editor at *The Irish Times*. Caroline I still miss, for her kindness, her gaiety, her irreverence and integrity.

autobiographical Shem the Penman episode of *Finnegans Wake*: 'He even ran away with hunself and became a farsoonerite, saying he would far sooner muddle through the hash of lentils in Europe than meddle with Irrland's split little pea.'

I arrived in Dublin towards the end of the McDaid Age, when the literary topers and talkers were on their last legs. I would see Behan and Kavanagh about the place. Behan,[*] for all his wild ways, lived in a fine handsome house on leafy Anglesey Road in Ballsbridge, safely beyond the southernmost limits of Baggotonia. Kavanagh, who by then was visibly dying, would sit for hours on the steps outside the house where my flat was[†] and glare at the basement offices of the Dolmen Press across the road—Dolmen was the major poetry publishing house of the day, run by Liam Miller, one of the unsung, or at least insufficiently sung, heroes of the time.[‡] Flann O'Brien-Myles na Gopaleen-Brian O'Nolan I encountered only once, when on a twilit autumn eve I spotted him wobbling his way down a deserted Grafton Street with hat askew and coattails flapping in the October gale, a sad, drink-sodden figure.

---

[*] Cicero, who saw much more of Behan than I ever did, judges him to have been a 'Bengal'—a chancer, that is, as in 'Bengal Lancer'. Among his many accomplishments, Cicero has a mastery of rhyming slang.

[†] I also spotted him one day in the window of Parsons bookshop; he was literally *in the window*, for he had climbed on to the sloped display shelf and was sitting there, elbows on knees, among, and on, the books laid out for sale, intently scanning the pages of the *London Magazine*. He was quite a sight, in his hobnailed boots, with his battered hat on the back of his head, mouthing disparaging comments and pretending not to notice the stares of the passers-by. At heart they were all show-offs, even the gruffest of them.

[‡] The other day on my shelves I came across a long-forgotten postcard-sized *Georgian Dublin: Twenty-Five Colour Aquatints by James Malton*, published by Dolmen, and with a foreword by—who else?—Maurice Craig. You see? Everything hangs together.

The city had more than its share of frauds, poseurs and poetasters. But there were genuinely talented people, not just artists but scholars, too, however eccentric, such as the historian and genealogist Eoin 'The Pope' O'Mahony and the folklorist Seamus Ennis. And we had genuine wits. Of these, my favourite, partly, I suppose, because I was lucky enough to know him a little, was the diplomat and journalist Seán Mac Réamoinn. I still remember his superb reports from Rome for Irish television on the Second Vatican Council between 1962 and 1965—'Of course, I wasn't in Rome at all,' he pretended to confide to me years later, his glossy eyes popping with suppressed mirth. 'It was all done in secret on a back lot in Hollywood.' As a liberal Catholic, Mac Réamoinn believed that John XXIII's Council would radically transform the Church, which it did, though not necessarily for the better.

I had lunch with him ten or so years ago—he died in 2007—in one of his favourite restaurants, the Unicorn on Merrion Row. He was suffering badly from emphysema and it was difficult for him to breathe. 'Don't make me laugh!' he would wheeze, clutching at his chest and rolling his eyes, his moustache bristling in comic distress. The likelihood of *my* making *him* laugh was remote, but by the end of our afternoon together certainly I had stitches in both my sides.

Bons mots when they are written down tend to lose their sharpness, but I cannot resist giving at least a few examples of Mac Réamoinn at his brilliant best. At the beginning of our lunch that day I asked him how he was—I was being polite, for it was plain he had not long to live—and he shook his head ruefully. 'I'm like the Census,' he said, 'broken down by age, sex and religion.' I recalled, too, a journalist colleague of his telling me how at the end of a late-night session in a Donnybrook pub Seán had risen regretfully to leave while there were drinks still on the table, saying, 'Well, I'm off home now to put my feet up in front of a roaring wife.' But surely his best line ever was an instant response when he heard someone repeating Cyril Connolly's famous assertion that 'Inside every fat man there is a thin man trying to get out.' 'Yes,' Seán said, 'and outside every thin girl there's a fat man trying to get in.'

Would the McDaidians all have been better advised to follow the example of so many of their artistic forebears and go into exile? It should be noted, by the way, that Irish writers never merely emigrated, they always 'went into exile'.

The city, like all cities, had its complement of eccentrics, but Dublin was so small that they seemed uncommonly numerous. Most of them were sad poor creatures, maimed in body or spirit or both, but a few there were who added appreciably to the gaiety of the town. The Hon. Garech Browne, of the family of Oranmore and Browne, whose mother was a Guinness, dressed in tweeds so rough and readymade that it seemed he must have woven them himself, and would arrive at the Shelbourne Hotel in top hat and cape, driving a coach and pair with heedless insouciance and flair. So flamboyant a sight was he, up there on the driving seat, that every time I saw him I wanted to cheer. He is still going strong, living in an enchanted castle at the foot of one of County Wicklow's hammered-steel lakes.

More colourful even than Garech was the mountainy man whom

I thought of as the Celtic Chieftain. Beaded, bearded and fearsomely unbarbered, he would tramp about the city wrapped in a rug and with a tartan blanket draped over his shoulders, bearing in his right hand a mighty staff a foot taller than himself and as thick as a strong man's forearm. He had, according to Cicero, a gaggle of similarly garbed maidens, who followed him wherever he went, mute with adoration, though them I never spied. He was a canny old boy, and charged tourists a fiver to photograph him. Where, I wonder, did he go to at night? Was there a cave somewhere, within a mossy grotto, in one of the city parks, where he and his maenads laid themselves down about a blazing fire to dream of ancient days?

· · · · ·

The Ireland of the McDaid Age was a hard, mean-spirited place for anyone with artistic ambitions. When I first visited eastern Europe in the early 1980s, at a time when the Cold War was extremely warm, I felt immediately, and horribly, at home: *they* had the Communist Party invigilating their lives from the cradle to the grave, while *we* had the Catholic Church doing exactly the same thing. As the English historian Hugh Trevor-Roper never tired of pointing out, Communism and Catholicism are but two sides of the same debased coin.

As in Budapest, Prague or Warsaw, so also was it in Dublin that the intelligentsia kept itself in some way going by a combination of

cunning circumspection and desperate humour. My late friend the novelist John McGahern used to give a mordantly funny account of the day he was sacked from his teaching job at Belgrove School in Clontarf, after his novel *The Dark* had been banned by the Censorship Board. He was called to the office of the principal, a bibulous cleric, who said to him: 'It's not the book, you know, that we minded most, but the fact that you had to bloody-well go off and marry a divorced woman, and a foreigner at that'—McGahern's first wife was a Finn, Annikki Laaksi—'while here at home the women's tongues are hanging out for a man.'

'Well,' McGahern answered drily, 'they weren't hanging out in *my* direction!'

Yes, it's funny, but the aftermath was not: John had to emigrate to England and work at odd jobs there, including on building sites. The wonder of it was that he harboured so little bitterness; he even returned, with his second wife, Madeline, to live in Ireland, not far from where he was born and brought up. Perhaps the sweetest memory I have of him is the day he took my wife and me to visit his favourite meadow, near his house on a lake in Foxfield, County Leitrim. 'Look at that,' he said, surveying the field of grasses and wild flowers, 'wouldn't that lift your heart?' Later he filled his cap with wild mushrooms and brought them back to the house for Madeline to cook.

I often wondered—I would not have dared to ask him the question outright—if in his life by the lake he did not sometimes hanker after the old Dublin days, but always I recalled the exchange between the poet Philip Larkin and an interviewer who asked him how it was that he had chosen to live in Hull in the north of England, 'so far away from the centre'. To this Larkin responded with one of his balefully owlish stares and asked: 'The centre of what?'

Even I, young as I was, did not imagine that Baggotonia, for all its dingy glamour, was the centre of anything much. I regarded the McDaids crowd with mild disdain and a measure of arrogant compassion—in fact I never, not once, crossed the threshold of that pub, preferring Neary's, one street further up, a civilised house that had, and still has—I checked the other day—four handsome, white-globed and *working* gas-jet lamps set at intervals along the bar.

The pubs were pretty much all we had: Dublin did not 'go in' for restaurants. There was Jammet's in Nassau Street, but no one could afford to dine there except visiting grandees or the odd film star, and of course Micheál and Hilton, if Lord and Lady Longford, their erstwhile mentors at the Gate Theatre—she as thin as a thrush, he as large as a smallish elephant—were paying the bill. The rest of us could just about manage an occasional beano at the Paradiso on Westmoreland Street—ten-and-six the Tournedos Rossini—or a ham sandwich and a glass of shandy at the Gresham Hotel or the Shelbourne's Horseshoe Bar, as dimly lit and pleasingly louche today as it was then.

In the early 1970s the late David Farrer, my editor at the London publishing house of Secker & Warburg, paid a visit to Dublin—he had come to see not me but Christy Brown, whose novel *Down All the Days* was about to make a fortune for the author and for Secker—and took my wife and me to dinner in the old Russell Hotel, long gone now, at the corner of Harcourt Street and St Stephen's Green. It was a very good dinner, so good that I remember still, all these years later, what I ate: fish soup to start, then ossobuco, followed by chocolate mousse. The cost of the wines that we drank—a bottle of Montrachet first, I think, and then a velvety St-Estèphe—was probably not much less than the advance that Secker had paid me for my first book. David was something of a legend in the trade—publishing still had living legends, then. During the war he had been private secretary to Lord Beaverbrook, and later wrote a memoir of the old monster, *G—for God Almighty.**

In his very first job, so he told us, he used to go to work on an elephant.

'Yes,' he said, obviously enjoying our baffled stares. 'I was tutor to an Indian prince, you see, and every morning at nine o'clock sharp an elephant and his mahout would arrive at my bungalow, and I would climb aboard the beast and trundle off to the palace. Remarkable creatures, elephants . . .'

Then he ordered a brandy for himself, but nothing for us. I was very low on the list, after all.†

---

* One day Beaverbrook was dictating an editorial to David over the telephone, and David, because of a poor connection, had to keep asking him to repeat a word, until finally His exasperated Lordship yelled down the line: '*Facing*: F for fool, A for ass, C for cunt, I for I, N for nothing and G for God Almighty!'
† My agent later explained to me David's hierarchical order: in London, small-fry such as myself were taken for a drink to the Coach and Horses in Greek Street, rising stars were given lunch at the Jardin des Gourmets, also on Greek Street, while Booker Prize shortlistees and the like were wined and dined at the Garrick Club.

Treats like that evening at the Russell were rare, if indeed there were any others like it—although now that I think of it there was also a memorable lunch at the Hibernian Hotel on Dawson Street to celebrate the publication of one of Jennifer Johnston's early novels. A publishing lunch! Now there's a thing of the past, like suspenders and post-prandial cigars. During that one at the Hibernian I had a sneezing fit caused by champagne bubbles getting up my nose. I also recall a very grand young woman, the publisher's wife, I think, who, hearing me comment sardonically on the splendours of our surroundings—the Hibernian really was sumptuous—enquired incredulously if by any chance I were, well, if I were a *socialist*. Before I had a chance to reply—what would I have said, I wonder?—she burst into hoots of happy laughter. Do I imagine it, or am I right in thinking that the English can never quite take the Irish seriously? When I am over there I have the impression that everyone I speak to is just about managing to keep a straight face.

At the other end of the scale from Jammet's, the Russell and the Hibernian was Gaj's restaurant in Baggot Street. Margaret Gaj, née Dunlop, was a woman before her time. She had been a Red Cross nurse in the war, and met and married a Polish soldier, Bolesław Gaj, and moved with him to Dublin, where, enterprising woman that she was, she opened a restaurant, first in Molesworth Street, within an olive stone's throw of the Hibernian, moving later to the heart of Baggotonia. Mrs Gaj, as everyone called her, would have known exactly how to answer the question the publisher's wife had facetiously put to me, and would have brooked no mocking laughter.

She was a vigorous left-wing activist, and a member of and mover in many of the social protest groups that sprang up in the 1960s. She was involved in the Dublin Housing Action Committee, which mounted street protests to demand improved housing for the poor, and was one of the founders of the Women's Liberation Movement in Ireland. Her restaurant was a haven of sanity, freedom and good cheer, and at half-a-crown, the bangers and chips were not only a bargain but also, as a friend of mine used to say, 'a great tightener'.

The best pub outside Baggotonia, the best pub in the city, in fact, was Ryan's of Parkgate Street, just below the main entrance to the Phoenix Park, a handsome and commodious house, overseen by Mr Ryan himself, tall, spare and sandy-haired, with a limp that made him seem to be poling himself along in an invisible gondola.* He wore a white shirt and a black waistcoat, and one of those long tubular black aprons that are still to be seen on Paris waiters. Well into the 1970s women were not allowed into the main bar of Ryan's. When one entered with one's girl, Mr Ryan, pursing his lips and giving a single and barely perceptible nod, would tug with his index finger on a length of twine that ran all the way down the room and was connected at the end to a spring-operated latch on the door of the snug: the door would open with a sort of confidential action, one would slip inside, the twine would be released and, click!, the door would snap shut, and there we were, as snug as one could only be in a snug.

---

* Cicero is able to tell me that the immensely dignified Mr Ryan had the unlikely nickname of 'Bongo'.

What were the drinks we drank? Guinness, certainly, great oceans of the stuff—though I never could develop a taste for it—and whiskey, by John Jameson & Son, and Powers, which was said to be smoother on the tongue than JJ&S; but never Scotch. For a while there was a vogue for Jamaican rum mixed with blackcurrant juice, which deposited a thick sweet scum on the roof of the mouth, the effortful removal of which left one's tongue aching at the root. Beers, too, soapy Smithwick's, insipid Carlsberg, and Bass, which was slightly disreputable, since in the 1930s this lowly working-man's tipple had been the main target of a republican campaign to boycott British goods in Ireland.

In the pubs where women were admitted they were not allowed to order pints. I have just remembered this, and am filled with wonderment. A woman could have two halves simultaneously, in two glasses, but not a pint in a pint glass. Where did this absurd rule come from, and why did we so meekly obey it? Under a tyrannical regime—and the Ireland of those days was a spiritual tyranny—the populace becomes so cowed that it does the state's work for it voluntarily. And as every tyrant knows, a people's own self-censorship is the kind that works best. In the 1990s, when revelations of clerical sexual abuse and the Catholic Church's cover-ups put an end to its hegemony almost overnight, my generation scratched its head and asked, in voices trembling with incredulity, 'How could we let them get away with it for so long?' But the question, of course, contained its own answer: *We let them get away with it*. Power is more often surrendered than seized.

Suppressed as we were, we sought our profane little pleasures wherever we could find them. For instance, everyone smoked, and went at it seriously, too, as if it were a duty. The brands we favoured were Player's, Gold Flake, Sweet Afton, in its lovely woodbine-coloured packet, and Woodbines themselves, though they were working-class and shunned by all but the poorest among us. For a while I took to Churchman's, which were very posh, and shifted sometimes, when I was in one of my more insouciant West-Brit phases, to Senior Service. In every pub, and at every party, a solid cube of tobacco smoke stood in the air and filled the room, cobweb-coloured, thick and unmoving. At closing time we would stumble out into the clammy darkness, coughing and wheezing, with palms pressed distressedly to heaving breastbones. After the fug of indoors the night was always a surprise, clean and cold and somehow disapproving of us and our half-drunken rowdiness. Torn newspapers and discarded chip-bags would roll along the middle of the road, like tumbleweed, and scavenging seagulls, surreally huge when seen close-up, would step away from us with disdainful delicacy, softly shrieking.

Recently an Italian friend of mine who lives and works in America came to Dublin to write an article on Ireland for a travel magazine. I met her on a summer day in the Winding Stair restaurant, at a window that looked out on a wintry scene of scudding clouds and a leaden Liffey. She had been strolling about the city for a couple of days, observing the people and dropping into pubs and hotel lounges. 'I have made a discovery,' she said. 'I have realised that alcohol is

for the Irish what sunshine is for the Latin peoples of the south.' I laughed, for it was a funny notion, but true, too, and profound, in its way. Even those of us who delight in the Irish climate, cherishing its lack of extremes and its exquisite, silvery, ever-changing light, must have something to warm us up and lift our spirits.

The alternative to pubs, although perhaps rather they were their complement, were the cinemas, or picture houses, as we still called them when we momentarily forgot our pretensions to social ascension. They were concentrated mostly in O'Connell Street and its surrounds. Their names had a sort of stately, antique grandeur: there was the Carlton, the Metropole, the Ambassador, the Adelphi, and, queen mother of them all, the Savoy, which could seat nearly three thousand picture-goers. What a sight it was, when the lights came up, to look about the great amphitheatre of the balcony and see so many dazed dreamers struggling to wake from the two-hour fantasy they had been mesmerised by as it floated and flickered across the enormous and enfolding CinemaScope screen. Film is the people's poetry, and it is in the picture house that we encounter, briefly, fleetingly, the latter-day gods of Olympus—stars, film stars!—impossibly beautiful, impossibly assured, flawless and wholly fake, just like the gods of old.

Although it was shabby and run-down by the 1960s, my favourite picture house was the Capitol, in Princes Street, the foyer of which stood at right angles to the old Princes Bar, one of Dublin's finest pubs, long gone now. The Capitol, built on the site of the *Freeman's Journal*, opened in 1920 and, besides a cinema, boasted a restaurant, a café, a bar and a ballroom. Performers who appeared live on stage there included Sophie Tucker—yes, Sophie Tucker!—John McCormack, W. C. Fields, Beniamino Gigli and Paul Robeson. The final live show was staged in 1953. The Capitol, like the Princes Bar, was pulled down long ago, and the street is now not much more than an unloading bay for cut-price stores roundabout.

The only cinema I knew of within the purlieus of Baggotonia was the Grafton Picture House—designed by Richard Orpen, the painter William Orpen's brother—on Triple-B Grafton Street. From the end of the 1950s onwards it showed only cartoons and newsreels, but it had a first-floor café, which was a fancy place in which to treat your girlfriend to afternoon tea. It was there that I had my first proper date with the first real, as distinct from fantasy, love of my life. Her name was Stephanie Delahaye. Ah, Stephanie, I have only to close my eyes—no, I don't even have to close them—and I can see the frail, pale back of your neck, dotted low down on the left with a tiny chocolate-brown mole, as you lean over your teacup, at a table by the railings; I imagine I can even hear the din of Grafton Street outside, where the sunlight rolls its golden hoops among the busy legs of passers-by.

In those pre-multiplex days the cinemas were each a single vast palace, neon-signed, plush-seated, kitsch-beyond-kitsch, patrolled by slick-haired commissionaires who would brook no nonsense from gurriers or their girls, and tended by middle-aged usherettes— wonderful word!—who wielded their flashlights like flaming swords, ever on the lookout for lewd goings-on in the back row, the scourge of litterers, and dauntless ejectors of the insolent and the obstreperous. At the intervals the crimson curtains—shades of the Kayser Bondor ladies' brittly gleaming gowns!—would swish shut, and in front of the stage, phosphorescently spot-lit, a fairy-like vision would appear, as if descended from the empyrean, in a skimpy skirt and a gay little hat tipped jauntily to one side, bearing a tray of tempting sweetmeats for sale: Mars bars, Cadbury's Dairy Milk, tiny tubs of HB ice cream with miniature wooden spatulas expertly clipped inside the lids, bags of popcorn, of Scots Clan toffees, of Lemon's Pure Sweets . . . Sugar in our mouths, and saccharine on the screen.

The erotic potential of the picture house was an open secret known to every male from late boyhood onwards. The films we were permitted to see were so severely butchered by the Censor's Office that what was left of them made little sense, and so we were largely free to ignore what was happening, or failing to happen, on the screen and concentrate instead on getting a hand—hands, even—inside our girlfriends' clothing. The most sought-after of the few zones permitted to us was that part of the upper leg bare above the stocking-top. This cushion of flesh—I should say these cushions, since after all there were two of them, though one was rarely if ever permitted to get at, and certainly not between, both of them—soft, plump and delightfully cool, taught me my first lesson in the entrancing aesthetics of the human body. Looking back now, in the late-autumn of life—or is it early winter?—I am convinced that art and the erotic are as closely entwined as a pair of lovers lying in each other's arms. I do not think I am being fanciful in this. The life of a young male is not often illumined by the spark of beauty. I believe that what my adolescent self—that poor poseur shivering in the cheap shoes of his emotions—wanted and hoped for in girls had less to do with lust than a yearning after the exquisite. Or perhaps I was just too soppy for words.

And girls, what were their desires? If I did not give the matter the consideration that I should have, I can comfort myself, a little, by reflecting that it is a question even Old Father Freud could not pretend to know the answer to—did he not himself ask, *What does a woman want?* But how did it feel to them, the girls, there in the flickering dimness of the back row of the stalls, to be pawed at with that combination of wheedling and menace in which young men— in which all men—specialise? Surely they were prey to a confused mixture of emotions—excitement and fear, longing and revulsion, desire and . . . what? Plain irritation, perhaps?

The first art-house cinema in the city was the Astor, on Eden Quay, which opened in the early 1950s with a showing of De Sica's *Bicycle Thieves.* Around the turn of the decade my cousin Mary B. and I used to travel up from Wexford—how? by train? bus?—and go to afternoon showings of New Wave films by Ingmar Bergman, Federico Fellini, François Truffaut, Luis Buñuel, Jean-Luc Godard, Alain Resnais . . . My favourite of them all was Michelangelo Antonioni, who, besides the mellifluous multisyllabics of his name, recommended himself to me by employing for his films the most elegant and attractive film stars in the world. I still recall the shock of baffled pleasure I experienced as I grappled with the unresolved, and probably irresolvable, enigmas of *L'Avventura*—remember the water spout? What a happy chance that was for a director, rising up, magical and menacing, out of the sea while a scene was in the process of being shot.

The star of *L'Avventura*, the sculptedly beautiful Monica Vitti, was the most longed-for among all my cinematic obscure objects of desire. I knew, even in those days of my small-town boyhood, that Antonioni's work was meant to be a searing existential indictment of the postwar capitalist West—but *Oh*, I used to think, sitting there on dusty plush with that exquisite creature's silver-and-soot image looming out over me from the Astor's little square screen, *oh, to be unhappy in the arms of Monica Vitti!*

Cupid is the god who lurks in all corners, waiting to pounce.

5

A Pisgah Sight
of Palestine

I N MARCH 1966, in the small hours of the morning, I was jolted out of sleep by a distant thud that was not so distant that it did not make the panes of my bedroom window rattle. I had never heard such a sound before, abrupt and oddly muted and somehow *sullen*, and I could not think what it might be that had caused it. *The isle is full of noises*, I thought dreamily, and fell back to sleep. In the morning the news was all over the radio and the newspapers. At 1.30 a.m., an explosion had demolished Nelson's Pillar, in the centre of O'Connell Street, the city's best-known landmark. That year was the fiftieth anniversary of the 1916 Rising, and the IRA, which had been dormant since the fizzling out of a desultory and often farcical bombing campaign along the border with Northern Ireland in the 1950s, had decided to mark the occasion with a 'spectacular', a word we would come to know, and dread, in later decades.

The Pillar, as it was known to everyone, was erected in 1809 in what was then Sackville Street, the developer Luke Gardiner's elegant Georgian boulevard, to celebrate Admiral Nelson's victory at the battle of Trafalgar four years earlier. A plaque laid with the foundation stone bore the legend:

BY THE BLESSING OF ALMIGHTY GOD, To Commemorate the Transcendent Heroic Achievements of the Right Honourable HORATIO LORD VISCOUNT NELSON, Duke of Bronti in Sicily, Vice-Admiral of the White Squadron of His Majesty's Fleet, Who fell gloriously in the Battle off CAPE TRAFALGAR, on the 21st Day of October 1805; when he obtained for his Country a VICTORY over the COMBINED FLEET OF FRANCE AND SPAIN, unparalleled in Naval History. This first STONE of a Triumphal PILLAR was laid by HIS GRACE CHARLES DUKE OF RICHMOND and LENNOX, Lord Lieutenant General and General Governor of Ireland, on the 15th Day of February in the year of our Lord, 1808, and in the 48th Year of our most GRACIOUS SOVEREIGN GEORGE THE THIRD, in the presence of the Committee appointed by the Subscribers for erecting this monument.

I admire the sonorously rolling periods here, but what I like most is the way in which the whole thing topples into bathos right at the end, when there pops up the 'Committee appointed by the Subscribers', a sudden mundanity upon which even capital letters cannot confer the hoped-for gravitas. I am reminded of the superb, mock-heroic closing lines of the Cyclops episode in *Ulysses*, when Leopold Bloom is forced to flee Barney Kiernan's public house on a jaunting car to escape the wrath of the ultra-nationalist and anti-Semitic 'Citizen', who flings a biscuit tin after him:

> When, lo, there came about them all a great brightness and they beheld the chariot wherein He stood ascend to heaven. And they beheld Him in the chariot, clothed upon in the glory of the brightness, having raiment as of the sun, fair as the moon and terrible that for awe they durst not look upon Him. And there came a voice out of heaven, calling: *Elijah! Elijah!* And he answered with a main cry: *Abba! Adonai!* And they beheld Him even Him, ben Bloom Elijah, amid clouds of angels ascend to the glory of the brightness at an angle of fortyfive degrees over Donohoe's in Little Green street like a shot off a shovel.

The Nelson monument was designed by the English architect William

Wilkins, but his plan was modified, for cost-cutting reasons, by Francis Johnston of Armagh, who also designed the General Post Office . . . Oh, dear: even as I write, how the overblown amplitudes of Joyce's lingo lingers! But onwards, onwards regardless!

Dubliners always had an ambiguous attitude to the Pillar. Republicans detested it, naturally, but for the rest of us it was merely a handy meeting point in the city centre, so rooted and so familiar that we hardly noticed it any more as an object in itself. In blowing it up the IRA had done a remarkably efficient job—probably as a result of British Army training, for many IRA men had enlisted with the enemy's forces to learn the skills of warfare—and the explosion caused minimal damage to surrounding buildings, mainly shattering the windows of shops and offices, although a taxi man parked nearby was lucky to escape with his life. 'The boys' had been thorough, certainly, but only half of the granite column had come down, and some days later engineers from the Irish Army were sent in to complete the demolition.

In 1969 the government introduced the somewhat comical-sounding Nelson Pillar Act, which wound up the trust that had been running the monument as a tourist attraction—for a modest fee one could gain access to a stairway inside the pillar, which led, after a hard and dizzying climb, to a viewing column at the top—and paid the trustees compensation for loss of earnings. Over the years various suggestions were made as to what should replace the Pillar, but nothing happened until 2003, when the Millennium Spire was driven deep into the heart of the site.

Reaction to the destruction of the Pillar was in general one of amusement. In those days the IRA was not taken seriously as a military or political force, but all the same people were impressed by the expertise and aplomb with which the operation had been carried out. The police investigation of the bombing seems to have been half-hearted. One report in an English newspaper claimed that six men had been arrested and questioned in connection with the incident, but if so they were never charged. There were rumours, too, that ETA, the Basque separatist movement, had come over and done the job as a training exercise. It was not until the year 2000 that a former IRA man, Liam Sutcliffe, claimed in an interview on Irish television that he and a group of what would now be called dissident republicans, led by one Joe Christle—whose 'recklessness' had led the IRA to expel him from its ranks—were the ones who had carried out 'Operation Humpty Dumpty', and that he it was who had planted the pre-timed bomb near the top of the monument. Sutcliffe was later questioned by the Gardaí, but no charges were brought against him.

Looking back now, past thirty years of tribal slaughter in Northern Ireland,* one breaks into a sweat at the thought of the casualties the Pillar bomb could have caused. At the time we just shrugged, or laughed; unregenerate children that we are, we glory in a little harmless

---

* And in the South, too, let us not forget: bombings in Dublin and Monaghan on 17 May 1974, carried out by the Ulster Volunteer Force, probably with the help of British security forces, killed thirty-three people and an unborn child; this was the deadliest co-ordinated massacre of the Troubles.

destruction now and then, happy to see bits of the adult world brought tumbling down. At the time a comic song, 'Up Went Nelson', cobbled together by a group of Belfast schoolteachers, was for weeks the best-selling record on the 'hit parade' south of the border.

The Pillar figures in one of the most intricate and more diverting episodes of Joyce's *Ulysses*, when Stephen Dedalus relates to a gathering of his newspaper cronies the tale of 'two Dublin vestals', who raid their moneybox to fund an outing to climb the monument and take a view of the city. With a little expansion and development the tale would have fitted perfectly into Joyce's sublime short-story collection *Dubliners*. Stephen titles his anecdote 'A Pisgah Sight of Palestine or the Parable of the Plums'. In it, Nelson is referred to as 'the onehandled adulterer,' a typical example of Stephen's many arch and deliberately unfunny formulations. Yet who could resist Joyce's marvellous fondness for the two adventuresses, and the warmth and accuracy of his invention? As Stephen relates it, the pair

> buy one and fourpenceworth of brawn and four slices of panloaf at the north city dining rooms in Marlborough street from Miss Kate Collins, proprietress . . . They purchase four and twenty ripe plums from a girl at the foot of Nelson's pillar to take off the thirst of the brawn. They give two threepenny bits to the gentleman at the turnstile and begin to waddle slowly up the winding staircase, grunting, encouraging each other, afraid of the dark, panting, one asking the other have you the brawn,

praising God and the Blessed Virgin, threatening to come down, peeping at the airslits. Glory be to God. They had no idea it was that high.

Cicero has a piece of the Pillar at home. He lives on the south Docks, at the mouth of the Grand Canal—if canals have mouths—in a former eighteenth-century grain warehouse that he and Mrs Cicero have turned into one of the most striking dwellings in the city. It is next door to the U2 studio, which he sold to the band; when the noise gets too loud, he tells me, he bangs his shoe on the wall to tell them to turn the volume down. He has been collecting things since he was a teenager. Incorporated into the wall of his living room is the stone lintel from the door by which Joyce's two intrepid virgins would have set off upon their aerial adventure.* On the lintel, Nelson's name is carved in handsome, gilded letters—or as a stone-mason would correctly say, Cicero informs me, the name is 'set in and picked out in gold'.

Today we are off to see the Admiral's head. It is a condition of these journeys of ours into Dublin's past that Cicero will never tell me beforehand where it is we are bound—'If I told you I'd have to

---

* It is reported that Wittgenstein, too, in his Dublin sojourn, made an ascent of the Pillar. It seems that he and his friend Dr Drury, like a pair of mitching schoolboys, bought a couple of cheap cameras in Woolworths and went up to stand in the Admiral's shadow and take panoramic shots of the city. I am reminded of a passage at the close of the *Tractatus*: 'My propositions serve as elucidations in the following way: anyone who understands me eventually recognises them as nonsensical, when he has used them—as steps—to climb up beyond them.'

kill you.' This lends to each occasion a sense of childish anticipation, to which the seven-year-old inside me responds as he used to when he walked through the darkness of those eighths of December on his way to the train and Percy Place and Clery's and the Palm Beach and . . . and happiness, that simplest of states an entrance to which is so difficult to effect.

As we settle ourselves in Cicero's eager little two-seater—*vroom vroom*—I turn over in my mind the question of where Horatio's noble head might be stored. Since the Pillar was so high—134 feet, or 40.8 metres, if you must know—I imagine the statue atop it to have been huge, so surely the head will be installed in, say, the ballroom of some once-magnificent townhouse in one of the grander Georgian squares. I have a happy image of myself posing beside it for my photograph, the thing as tall as I am, and I with my elbow nonchalantly propped against the hero's stone ear. But why, then, are we in the further reaches of non-B Pearse Street? Cicero is an admirable and invaluable guide, but there are times when a vagueness as to exact locations settles upon him. We have to make no fewer than three U-turns, in the middle of hooting traffic, before we at last draw to a sudden and, to me, unexpected halt in front of . . . the Pearse Street public library.

I was very young when I first fell in love with libraries. Frequently in my dreams I find myself revisiting the Wexford County Library, which nowadays is housed in a large and handsome modern building in Mallin Street just up from the North Station, the starting point of my long-ago December birthday trips, but in my time was located in the heart of the extravagantly mock-Gothic County Hall. One entered this crenellated pile along a wide and echoing linoleum-laid corridor, climbed a vast stone staircase and pushed open a heavy wooden door, and there it was, a cosy Paradise smelling of floor polish, the sun-bleached spines of books, and Miss Annette Flushing's all-pervading perfume.

Miss Flushing, blonde, pink and bespectacled, was one of three assistant librarians. She stood behind her counter at a raised level, so that when I approached her to have my week's borrowings stamped I would find myself at eye-level with her magnificent conical breasts poking against a pale-blue angora jumper; I know, I know, she must have worn other kinds of things too, blouses and such, but it's that particular jumper I see her inveterately in. I am sure I would have fallen in love with her, another of my phantom darlings, had her bust been less intimidating.

Miss Flushing was, like the rest of the staff, unfailingly kind, helpful and, in my case, sympathetic. I'm not sure why I should have seemed in need of sympathy, but even the head librarian, a silver-haired and slightly dotty old dear, tended me as if I were suffering from an obscure, chronic disorder, listening carefully to my enquiries and replying to them slowly and softly, and often stepping down from behind the counter to lead me to this or that shelf where the book I needed was stored; it seems to me they even stamped my borrowings with a special restraint and gentleness. But perhaps this is what all frequenters of the place thought. Perhaps they all imagined they were regarded as unique, all frail sufferers from the same disease that affected me, all ailing bibliomanes being treated for addiction, as in a literary methadone clinic, by Miss Flushing and her colleagues.

One of those colleagues was a handsome, dark-suited young man who liked to chat to me, not at all patronisingly, about books and authors, and who one day even lent me his own copy of Alberto Moravia's *Two Women*, which had fallen victim to the Censorship Board. When I had enquired after it Miss Flushing had given a snorting laugh—she had very large, shapely white teeth, the upper front ones always lightly flecked with lipstick—but my friend, behind her, had beckoned to me, and led me through the door at the back of the room and down the fire escape to the car park and to his car, and there had taken the book from the glove compartment and, glancing over one shoulder and then the other, had slipped the orange-covered Penguin paperback into my hands with a conspiratorial wink.

The Censorship Board was aided in its work by self-appointed guardians of the country's collective purity, sharp-eyed vigilantes who trawled through the public libraries in covert search of smut. In Graham Greene's *The Power and the Glory*, one of his more queasily religiose melodramas, the protagonist is a 'whiskey-priest' who has a daughter by a former mistress. In the Wexford County Library's copy of the book the name of the daughter had been scratched out—not cut out, but abraded from the surface of the page by the very careful use of a sharp blade; just the name was suppressed, mind, leaving a bare translucent patch in the paper, as if a mere name could be a blasphemy that no right-thinking reader should be allowed to see. Imagine: someone had checked out the book, taken it home, and sat for hours over this demented task, and then returned the volume to the library, basking no doubt in the satisfaction of having diligently carried out another small but vital part of the Lord's unresting and eternal work.

I am embarrassed to confess that I sinned once myself, in that library: I stole a book. It was the *Collected Poems* of Dylan Thomas — like many another swooningly bookish adolescent, I considered Thomas to be one of the major poets of the age — in a handsome hardback edition, bound in matt black buckram, and published by the grand old house of J. M. Dent & Sons. I had coveted the volume for months, and at last I could resist no longer: I hid it at the back of one of the shelves in the poetry section, waited six long weeks to see if anyone would disturb it, then stowed it under my coat and skulked out, my hands shaking in fright at the daring of the deed and my face on fire for the shame of it. I'm sure that when the loss was finally noticed the staff knew very well who the thief was, but if they did, they never challenged me. To ease my conscience, I have left a small legacy in my will as reparation to the library. I wonder which books they will buy with the money. Not mine, I trust.

Pearse Street Library, or the Dublin City Library and Archive, to give it its full flourish, is a venerable institution, and unusual in that it is housed in a handsome nineteenth-century building, which was designed specifically for the purpose it serves — as in all former colonies, most public institutions in Ireland occupy buildings that have been adapted, often incongruously, from what they were originally intended to be. It is well-stocked and lovingly run—was it my imagination or did I glimpse in the eyes of the two librarians on duty the day I visited there the same expression of sympathy and concern lavished upon me by Miss Flushing and her colleagues in the County Hall all those years ago? I suppose lovesickness for books is a malady that every librarian can diagnose straight off.

Cicero and I took the lift to the Reading Room. What a balm it is, the tranquillity that reigns in the reading room of a library!

'Ah,' Cicero said, 'there's Mr Nelson. Let's go and have a word.'

Idiotically, I looked about for the person who I supposed would be the head librarian, or the like, instead of which, all I saw was a stone head. And not the great five-foot-tall thing I had expected, either, for it is only slightly larger than life-sized. It stands on a modest plinth in a corner of the Reading Room, ravaged of expression, as is only to be expected—the doughty fellow was blown sky-high, after all. He has been weathered to a hollow-eyed and slack-mouthed starkness; a noticeable feature, or lack of feature, is his missing nose, which, it is said, was shot off by a stray bullet during the 1916 Rising. All in all he looks like a badly battered prize-fighter. He has hair, somewhat surprisingly, which must mean that the sculptor, one Thomas Kirk of Cork, left him hatless up there under the elements.

Incongruity, as we know, is one of life's abiding conditions. That I should be standing on a summer afternoon in Dublin City Library viewing the torsoless stone head from a statue to the victor of Trafalgar that fifty years before had been blown off its column in the middle of the night by a gang of IRA wildmen might not be said to rank among the more egregiously unlikely conjunctions I have experienced in my time, but, still, it felt bizarre in the extreme. Borges somewhere remarks how the surface of reality now and then and here and there reveals a tiny crack through which for an instant we catch a glimpse of the possibility of an entirely other order of things. My encounter with Admiral Nelson certainly opened one of those fissures.

And here, while I think of it, is another example of how sometimes the cat of contingency is let out of the world's seemingly seamless bag. As I said earlier, when I wrote *Christine Falls*, the first of my Benjamin Black books, I set my hero to live in a fancied-up version of the flat in Mount Street where I used to visit my Aunt Nan in the 1950s and which later I lived in myself. The designers of the English edition of the book, which was to be published by Picador, chose for the jacket illustration a very atmospheric photograph from the eighty million—yes, eighty million—still photographs available from the American stock photo agency Getty Images. The picture, probably taken in the 1950s, is of a woman walking along a short, gently sloping cobbled street under an archway, through which can be seen a continuing street, at the misty far end of which there are the jumbled backs of some tall narrow houses. I liked the photograph, and thought it perfectly suited to the period and 'feel' of the book. Also the scene struck me as faintly familiar, but I could not say why.

A little while later, on a visit to New York, I called in to see my editor John Sterling at Henry Holt, the American publisher of

Benjamin Black, which has offices in the Flatiron Building, that striking—and startlingly modern-looking—wedge of concrete and glass on downtown Fifth Avenue. John was aware of the photograph that Picador had chosen for the cover of *Christine Falls*, and was able to show me another book that Holt had recently published, an anonymous diary from Berlin at the end of the war, which, to my surprise, featured on its jacket the same Getty Images photograph of the woman walking down the cobbled street. It was, John and I agreed, a nice coincidence, peculiar and, like all coincidences, also a little eerie, even a little unnerving.

Picador duly published *Christine Falls*, and so attractive and so apt was the jacket illustration that a number of other European publishers, including Kastaniotis in Athens, decided to use the same photograph for their editions of the same book. When the Kastaniotis version was published the following year, my Greek editor and friend, the late Anteos Chrysostomides, came over to Dublin to make a television documentary on me and on my work. He was curious to see some of the parts of Dublin that had figured in the book, and of course I brought him first to Mount Street, Quirke's stamping ground, and mine, too, of old. It was Sunday, and the street was deserted. A little way along it, Anteos halted suddenly and pointed to the left. 'Look,' he said. 'It's the street from the photograph!'

And so it was, and there it was: Stephen's Place, which, under an archway and over cobbles, leads down from Upper to Lower Mount Street. Over the years I had passed by the spot countless

times, yet, amazingly, had not recognised it in the photograph. Far more amazing, however, was the fact that the Picador designers had managed to choose for the jacket, entirely by chance, from those millions of photographs available through Getty Images, one that had been taken in Upper Mount Street, where the book's fictional protagonist had his flat, and showing a scene that Quirke, like me, would have walked past every day.

Some years ago, at a dinner party in Barcelona, I was assured, by four statisticians who happened to be among the guests, that there is no such thing as a coincidence. They were right, of course, those four counters upon the abacus. But all the same . . .

And here, just for the fun of it, is another one of those coincidences that cannot be coincidences. I was invited to Zürich to give a reading at the James Joyce Centre there, run by Fritz Senn, the most charming and certainly the wittiest Joyce scholar I know— and I know a few, believe me. I did my reading in the evening, and next morning, as I was setting off to the airport to catch a midday flight home, Fritz presented me with a Xeroxed copy of a sonnet by my namesake, the nineteenth-century French poet Théodore de Banville, in which occurred the line *Les lauriers sont coupés*, which is also the title of the novel by Edouard Dujardin, which Joyce said had inspired in him the idea for the 'stream of consciousness' technique he used in *Ulysses*. Here was another nice little string of connections, and a fitting memento of my visit to the Centre, and of its hospitable director, whose acquaintance I had been so happy to make.

I flew back to Dublin, and later that afternoon was crossing the street in Sandymount when an old friend whom I had not seen for some years happened to be passing by in his motor car. He slowed the car and rolled down the window, and called out to me, 'I've been reading the Goncourt *Journals*, and they're *full* of mentions of Théodore de Banville!' He drove on, I continued to the other side of the road, and as I stepped on to the pavement there a woman tapped me on the shoulder and said, 'My good friend Fritz Senn tells me you gave a wonderful reading at the Joyce Centre last night!'

So, yes, it's true, there is no such thing as a coincidence.

· · · · ·

My tête-à-tête with Horatio's head is only the first of the day's adventures that Cicero has planned for us. For our next destination we shall cross to the north side of the city, and be plunged there into two very different versions of the past, laid layer and layer upon each other in the same house. Fording the river Liffey is a traumatic experience for any southsider. 'Did you get your visa sorted?' Cicero enquires of me, as we head towards the river, buzzing along Pearse Street, where the two-seater turns many an envious head. Vintage cars never lose their allure.

Luke Gardiner (1690-1755) was a master of the universe *avant la lettre*. He sprang, the youngest of five sons, from humble origins, but 'sprang' is the word, for soon he was buying up swathes of the city, including almost all of St Mary's Abbey estate, in the Jervis

Street area, which made him the biggest land owner north of the river. He also did what every aspiring gentleman did in those days, and made a good marriage. The wife he took was Anne Stewart, daughter of the Honourable Alexander Stewart, whose father was William Stewart, Viscount Mountjoy of County Tyrone. Gardiner's first big development, which he embarked on in the 1720s, was Henrietta Street, which starts from Bolton Street and ends smack up against the back gate of the King's Inns.* In the second third of the eighteenth century Henrietta Street was one of the most fashionable addresses in Georgian Dublin,† and number three was, according to Cicero, one of the handsomest houses in Ireland and, indeed, in Britain.

The house stands on what was originally a plot of land, possibly a garden, attached to number four, owned by John Maxwell, Member of Parliament for County Cavan and later Lord Farnham. In 1754 Maxwell's daughter married Owen Wynne of Sligo, an MP like his father-in-law, and, also like him, 'the descendant of opportunists', according to the splendid and invaluable online site *Irish Aesthete* — its wittily defiant motto: 'This is not an Oxymoron'—who either

---

* Christine Casey observes that the 'cold-shouldering' of Henrietta Street by the King's Inns is 'particularly apparent', and she is certainly right. The Inns, built on what was once the prettily named Plover Field, squats in all its stony majesty at the top of the street like a gigantic, misshapen, bloated and ornately bedizened frog. It looks much, much better from the other side, facing Constitution Hill. It was built by that genius James Gandon, after all.

† Maurice Craig tells us that in 1792 the Dublin Directory 'gives one Archbishop, two Bishops, four peers and four M.P.s (one a peer's eldest son)' as residing there.

bought or was given, perhaps as a wedding gift, the next-door plot, and on it built what became number three Henrietta Street.

The house is badly dilapidated. The brickwork of the façade is seriously spalled—another of the many new words Cicero has taught me on these jaunts of ours—and indoors all of the rooms are in a sorry state, although in some cases a surprising amount of the ceiling plasterwork remains more or less intact. The decline of Henrietta Street began when the King's Inns was built and many of the houses were bought up and transformed into solicitors' offices.* The foundation stone of the Inns was laid in 1800, the year of the Act of Union—strictly speaking, the Acts of Union, since there were two Acts combined in one—which amalgamated the Kingdom of Great Britain and the Kingdom of Ireland into the United Kingdom of Great Britain and Ireland, and which was, and in some quarters continues to be, the cause of much anger, woe and strife on this so often unhappy island.

Since the middle of the previous century the northside grandees had been steadily moving southwards across the river, following in the wake of the Earl of Kildare, and creating a new Georgian Dublin in the area around Leinster House—that's right: Baggotonia—and now, with the dissolution of the Irish Parliament, such as it was—its membership was restricted to Anglican Protestants—many English landlords in Ireland sold up and moved to 'the mainland', that is,

---

* Diarmuid Ó Gráda notes that 'by the 1760s the city had a thousand attorneys and the number continued to grow. There were half as many again by the end of the century.'

England. By the late 1800s, the liberal lawyer Tristram Kennedy, a reformist land agent during the famines of the 1840s, who built national schools and founded the Carrickmacross lace industry, had bought up three-quarters of the street for letting to his legal colleagues. Thus, thanks to Kennedy, evidently a decent fellow and a careful landlord, the fabric of the street was largely preserved up to the 1880s. By the close of the following decade, however, after Kennedy's death in 1885, much of his property had been acquired by a former Lord Mayor of Dublin, Joseph M. Meade. It was this execrable rack-renter—or provider of 'social housing', as he might be thought of today—who ordered the houses he owned in Henrietta Street to be divided up into a warren of separate rooms, to accommodate as many of the city's teeming poor as possible. Thus the street was turned into a slum.

Cicero and I are met at number three by a friendly estate agent who has agreed to allow us a quick tour of the house. We are given hard hats and luminous-yellow safety jackets. Original fixtures, including staircases and fireplaces, Cicero tells me, were torn out and sold in London—more of Alderman Meade's handiwork—but as we climb from one storey to the next, the magnificence of the house as it once was is evident on all sides. There are original field-panelled doors—'Run your hand over that wood,' Cicero urges me. 'Can't you feel the quality, the craftsmanship?'—while very soon I develop a crick in my neck from gazing up at the not quite ruined beauty of the plaster ceilings. What impresses most immediately, however, is the grand proportioning of the house. Each room has its

own character, its own distinction. This is a building that was built to be lived in graciously—even, it might be said, aesthetically.

In one of the bedrooms we spot a tiny piece of original wallpaper, still pasted in place. It is pale-grey with a design of delicate, feather-like fronds of some to me unidentifiable plant. Suddenly, as in Mrs Hanly's garden on the Vico Road, I am transported back to the Bay of Naples, and to Herculaneum, another of the towns, along with Pompeii, that were destroyed by the eruption of Mount Vesuvius in 79 AD. Unlike Pompeii, which was engulfed by a lava flow, Herculaneum was buried in volcanic dust, which preserved many of the town's fine houses and much of their interiors, including intricately tessellated floors, vividly tinted marble-clad walls, exquisitely detailed murals . . .

Herculaneum perished a very long time ago, yet much of its glory endures. Why should I wonder that this fragment of wallpaper has survived a mere three centuries? And yet I do, I do wonder. How many strata of time am I spanning here, how many imbricated layers of the past am I standing on? Italy of the ancients, Georgian Dublin, Sean O'Casey's tragic tenements . . .

'Isn't it amazing?' Cicero murmurs, touching a fingertip to the scrap of paper on the wall. 'Isn't it *amazing*?'

6

The Girl
in the Gardens

I FIRST SAW PARIS when I was eighteen. It was a good age at
which to celebrate such a momentous epiphany. At eighteen
one is grown-up enough to be not overly alarmed by the great
world's wonders yet young enough to register them with fresh-eyed
openness. When I say I *saw* Paris I mean it literally, for I spent almost
all of my time there out of doors. The shabby little hotel on the rue
Molière where I rented a fifth-floor *chambre de bonne* discouraged
guests from hanging about the place during the daytime, and I could
not afford long restaurant lunches or to lounge for hours in Left
Bank cafés. And so I walked and looked, and looked and walked.

What impressed me straight off and most strongly were the statues. In Ireland we tend to erect tremendous plinths and set upon them tiny figurines, our aspirations to *gloire* seeming to falter at an ascending rate. In Paris, however, those vast stone figures confront us imperiously, overwhelming in their scale, their grandeur, their vividness. From that long-ago visit I recall in particular venturing for the first time into the Jardin du Luxembourg. It was an afternoon in September, the great trees were dappled with sunlight the colour of straw and a hazing of fine blonde dust drifted in the air. Watching the bourgeoisie in self-conscious promenade, the dreamily strolling lovers, the children at play, I felt that I had stepped into a painting by Renoir or Raoul Dufy, or even one of Watteau's *fêtes galantes*.

Years later I used to stay sometimes in a friend's apartment near the Luxembourg Garden, and would take my daughter there in the afternoons. She was a toddler at the time, and delighted in the place, with its great trees and barbered lawns, its marble balustrades, its ponds and fountains. Now and then she would halt in front of one of those outsized noble statues and peer up at it with a mixture of awe and enquiry, as if the figure had called out to her and caught her attention, as they had caught mine, so many decades ago. Now she is grown-up and living in Paris, and the Luxembourg is one of her favoured haunts.

We have been accustomed to them for so long that we forget what a remarkable invention parks and pleasure gardens are. Although they are as old as antiquity—think of the Hanging Gardens of Babylon—parks are the quintessential public manifestation of the

Enlightenment and its values. If Andrew Marvell wrote not only 'The Garden' but also 'The Mower against Gardens', Alexander Pope saw the polite cultivation of sward and hedge as fit work for a species bent on achieving its apotheosis by way of control and bounded elegance. Brute nature must be tamed in the cause of good manners. The park-maker's aim is to soothe and civilise. Manhattan's Central Park, Hyde Park in London and Paris's Bois de Boulogne must surely be among the most expensive tracts of real estate ever given over to the pursuit of leisure.

Grandeur, however, is all very well, but I suspect each one of us has some more modest, secret place in which to wander and delight. When I first lived in Dublin, I found that instead of admiring the architecture I gravitated most frequently towards the city's parks, I suppose out of a muted or even unconscious nostalgia for my rural roots. There was, first and foremost, the Phoenix Park, a great sprawling semi-wilderness—although, as Maurice Craig cautions, it is not so 'natural' as it looks—that runs along the north bank of the Liffey. At 1,752 acres in all, it is bigger than London's Hyde Park, Regent's Park, Kensington Gardens, St James's Park, Green Park, and Greenwich and Battersea Parks *all put together*. Both Craig and Casey assure us that the name has nothing to do with the mythical bird that rises from the ashes of itself, but is derived from the Irish name for a spa well, *fionn uisce*, that rose in the vicinity.

The foundation of the park was the work of that most remarkable Irishman, James, Duke of Ormonde, or to give him his full title, James FitzThomas Butler, 1st Duke of Ormonde, 12th Earl of Ormond, 5th

Earl of Ossory, 1st Marquess of Ormond, 1st Earl of Brecknock, KG. The Butlers were one of the great English families in Ireland, and had been lords of the south-east of the country since the time of the Norman invasion of Ireland in the twelfth century. James's father, Viscount Thurles, was a Catholic, and his son, born in 1610, was brought up in that faith until a series of deaths put him in direct line of succession. At that point James I of England, determined that the Butler heir should be a Protestant, ordered that he be sent to live in the household of George Abbot, Archbishop of Canterbury. Later, when he was Lord Lieutenant of Ireland, the Duke's religion made him suspect among the Ormonde clan, the majority of whom were still of the Romish faith. However, his early years as a Catholic left him well-disposed, or at least not ill-disposed, towards the Catholic population in Ireland. He was serious about his Irishness, and as a young man in London took the unusual step, unusual that is for a man of his breeding and position, of learning at least a smattering of the Irish language, which later would come in useful when he was appointed to be a main force in British rule over this country.

· · · · ·

It would seem that Ormonde did not much care for the viceroy's official residence, Phoenix House, built some time in the early 1600s, and seems not to have lived there. Christine Casey describes it as 'a relatively modest building' and an 'aggrandised lodge'. In its expanded form the house today is Áras an Uachtaráin, where our President lives when he or she is in office. The story is told—ah, this city of stories!—that one of its past residents, whom patriotic piety forbids me to identify, coped with the tedium of the job by frequent recourse to the bottle. One night after a particularly vinous dinner Mr President, who went in terror of the termagant Mrs President, sat up late in his cups and, in need of a pee and unwilling to alert the missus to his drunken state, slipped outside and set to relieving himself against the trunk of a sheltering oak. The night was dark, and one of the sentries, new to his post, spotted the shadowy figure and called out a nervous 'Who goes there?' to which His Excellency replied with an oath. Again the sentry uttered his challenge, more loudly this time, and was again answered with another and equally loud expletive. The soldier was levelling his rifle preparatory to firing when his commanding officer came upon the scene, and luckily recognised the President. All deaths are tragic, of course, yet one cannot but muse wistfully on what the morning's headlines would have been, had the President been shot *in flagrante* by one of his own appointed guardians.*

Far finer than the Áras, in my uninformed opinion, is the house opposite, called Deerfield, which in the days of British rule was the chief secretary's lodge and since 1927 has been the American ambassador's residence. I have only been to the house once, in the late 1970s, during the enlightened term of Ambassador William Shannon and his wife Elizabeth. I can't remember what the occasion

---

* *The Daily Bleat*: PISSED AND PISSING PRES PLUGGED IN PARK.

was, but I do recall that there were many writers there—Bill Shannon was himself a writer and journalist—so many indeed that the playwright and novelist Tom Kilroy, looking about the room, remarked thoughtfully that if at that moment a bomb were to go off, pretty well the entire contemporary Irish literary world would have been wiped out on the spot. Think of *those* headlines . . .

Deerfield was built in 1776 for Sir John Blaquiere, of whom it was said that he 'has a good cook and good wines and knows their influence'. The same was true of Bill Shannon, but only in part. That evening we were served a very fine dinner, but where the wines were concerned, the ambassador seemed to know very little about their influence, with the inevitable result; I think everyone in the place was drunk, except Bill and Elizabeth. Jimmy Carter was coming to the end of his accident-prone presidency, and I recall my wife, at a late hour in the festivities, addressing Mrs Shannon with undiplomatic candour to enquire of her: 'And tell me, Elizabeth, what will you and Bill be doing after the election?'

Strange to think that Carter is still going strong, and doing good works worldwide, while poor Bill Shannon has been dead this thirty years.

• • • • •

It can be said that the Duke of Ormonde was one of the founders of modern Ireland. As Maurice Craig remarks, when the Duke returned here in 1662 after the Restoration of Charles II, 'the Renaissance, in a word, had arrived in Ireland'. That arrival was particularly significant for Dublin. According to Catherine Casey, 'Ormond's [*sic*] tenure as viceroy (1662-9, 1677-85) coincided with a remarkably sophisticated episode in the physical evolution of the city.' Maurice Craig describes him as 'a unique figure in modern Irish history', with few rivals 'in aristocratic ease, splendour, tolerance, flexibility and common sense'.*

However, lest we should fall into the easy error of over-estimating Ormonde's sunny disposition towards his former co-religionists, and towards Ireland in general—as Oliver Cromwell pithily put it, 'He who stops being better stops being good'—we must recall that he supported his mentor the lord deputy, Thomas Wentworth, Earl of Strafford, in his policy of confiscating large tracts of Catholic-owned land with the twin objects of swelling the coffers of the Crown and destroying the already much-diminished power of the Catholic gentry. This, of course, enraged the Ormonde clan, and was one of the resentments that led it to take up arms against English rule.

In the end Strafford fell from grace disastrously, indeed fatally— he was executed in the Tower of London in 1641—and Ormonde found himself leader of the Crown forces in Ireland, fighting first

---

* He was also possessed of a dry wit and a keen sense of irony. When he was in exile in France in the 1650s, a friend of his, a Scotsman and a fellow refugee, quarrelled with his French host and came to Ormonde for advice on what to do, since there was no one else in the city who would take him in. Ormonde advised that he should go back to his host and first eat his words, and then eat his dinner.

against the Irish rebels, Ormondes among them, and later, having made a pact with the Irish Confederates, against the Parliamentary invaders. Cavalier losses were no fault of his, but nevertheless in 1647 he had to surrender Dublin to the Roundheads, under terms that were supposed to protect Royalist Protestants and Catholics who had not taken part in the rebellion.

Eventually Ormonde was forced into exile in France, where he experienced extreme poverty: unable to afford a carriage or even a horse, he had to go about everywhere on foot. This period of his life reads like a chapter straight out of Henry Fielding or Alexandre Dumas—or even Laurence Sterne. In 1658 he returned from France to England—accompanied by one Daniel O'Neill, whom I should like to know a little more about, though all I have is his name—charged with sounding out the possibility of a Royalist Restoration. Going under the name of Pickering, Ormonde travelled in disguise, and finding it irksome to wear a wig at all times he discarded it and tried to dye his auburn hair black, with the result that it ended up in 'a variety of colours'.

Another stranger-than-fiction episode in the career of this extraordinary man occurred in 1670. There was about at that time an adventurer and ruffian with the wonderfully Hollywoodish name of Colonel Blood. Born in County Clare, Thomas Blood was the son of a blacksmith who had come up in the world. During the English Civil War the younger Blood first of all fought on the side of the King, but later turned his coat and joined forces with the Roundheads. For this piece of treachery he was granted large estates in Ireland, but he lost them after the Restoration. Badly in need of funds, he decided on the harebrained scheme of storming Dublin Castle and kidnapping Ormonde, then lord lieutenant, and holding him for ransom. The wily Ormonde learned of the plot, however, and laid a trap for Blood and his henchmen at the Sheep Street entrance to the Castle. Blood in his turn got wind of Ormonde's ruse, and fled to Northern Ireland, where he was first sheltered by the Presbyterians and then by the Catholics, among whom he passed himself off as a priest. Later he went to Holland, then joined a rebellion in Scotland, returned briefly to Dublin, and thence moved to London. There he formed a plan to assassinate Ormonde, his old enemy, though the commission for the disposal of the duke may have come secretly from Ormonde's rival at court, George Villiers, Duke of Buckingham.

Having been dismissed as Viceroy to Ireland, Ormonde at the time was back in London. He was travelling in his carriage up St James's Street one night after dining with the Prince of Orange when Blood sprang his desperate, and farcical, assault. Here is Maurice Craig's account of the incident:

> Blood and his son took the Duke out of his carriage and set him upon one of their own horses, and away with them down Piccadilly. Fortunately for Ormonde, nothing would satisfy the Colonel but to hang him on Tyburn tree. So he left his prisoner in charge of one of his men, while he himself went ahead to adjust the rope. By the time he came back to collect his victim, Ormonde

and the guard were struggling together on top of the horse, which was making off towards Knightsbridge. By the time help arrived, they had fallen off the horse into the mud, where they were rolling over and over together. The Colonel, seeing that the neighbourhood was by now well roused, fired a couple of shots at the Duke (but missed him) and galloped off into the night.

Blood continued in his wild ways, and notably made an attempt to steal the Crown Jewels from the Tower of London. He was aided in the botched theft by his brother-in-law, one Hunt, and a rascal with the Shakespearian name of Parrot, whose task it was to hide the Royal Orb by stuffing it down the front of his trousers. The affair ended in disaster, as usual, and the trio was captured in possession of the crown and the, presumably concealed, orb. However, King Charles, to everyone's astonishment, including probably the miscreant's, not only pardoned Blood, but gave him back his Irish estates, which had an annual yield of five hundred pounds. One can imagine Ormonde's feelings when he heard this news.*

---

* Blood had the dubious honour of being commemorated in verse by no less a poet than the rebarbative Earl of Rochester, who in his *History of Insipids* wrote:

> *Blood, that wears treason in his face,*
> *Villain complete in Parson's gown,*
> *How much he is at court in grace*
> *For stealing Ormond and the crown!*
> *Since loyalty does no man good,*
> *Let's steal the King, and outdo Blood!*

In 1662, on his return to Ireland after the Restoration, Ormonde, along with Sir Maurice Eustace, the lord chancellor, set to work immediately on the creation of the Phoenix Park. Christine Casey writes: 'The single most impressive legacy of vice-regal patronage in Dublin is the vast and varied landscape of the Phoenix Park, the largest enclosed city park in Europe.' As early as December 1662 Ormonde had persuaded Charles II to authorise the purchase from Eustace of four hundred acres of costly land north of the Liffey—as Maurice Craig remarks, 'Eustace's motives were quite evidently less pure than Ormonde's. By 1669, when Ormonde's viceroyalty was ended, the park had cost £31,000, and eventually would cost half as much again.'

Ormonde intended the Park ostensibly as a royal deer-park, and not merely as a grand demesne surrounding the vice-regal lodge. Emissaries were sent to England to purchase a herd of deer, and game birds were also fetched from across the water, while Lord Ossory, Ormonde's son, collected pheasants from the family estates. However, the Park was also to be, from the first, a place of leisure where the public at large might disport itself, and did. There were passages of peril in the early life of the Park, the most serious of which occurred when Charles II decided on a whim to give it as a gift to his mistress, the notorious Barbara Palmer, Duchess of Cleveland, a member of the same Villiers family from which had sprung Ormonde's enemy the Duke of Buckingham. Between them, however, Ormonde and Eustace succeeded in having the patent of ownership quashed.*

·　·　·　·　·

A glory to the city though the Phoenix Park may be, somehow I never felt at home there; or perhaps, on the contrary, I felt too much at home, vaguely seeing in the place a too close likeness to the fields and wooded slopes surrounding the hometown I had lately left behind. On the other hand, St Stephen's Green, in the Super-plus-B Georgian heart of Dublin, was more to my taste, with its suave charms such as Pope would have approved; yet at the same time it seemed to me, in its altogether too well-tended stateliness, deserving of Marvell's mower's complaint that

> 'Tis all enforced, the fountain and the grot,
> While the sweet fields do lie forgot

The Iveagh Gardens, not far from St Stephen's Green, are modest, not richly appointed, and wear an air of faint sadness; they suit me, though, and of all the parks in Dublin I like this one best. However, I am not sure I would have found the Gardens by myself, discreetly sequestered as they are behind the great grey cliff of what used to be University College Dublin and is now the National Concert Hall.[†] I

---

* Craig: '. . . the lady was placated with lands in England (for a wonder); but not before she had hissed at Ormonde that she hoped she might live to see him hanged. The Duke replied sweetly that for his part he was content to live to see her grow old.'

† For this imposing pile Christine Casey has only a frown: 'So great is the bulk and planar simplicity of this building that even the brightest sunlight barely alters its saturnine demeanour.'

was introduced to the place by a girl whom at the time I was busy falling in love with, in vain, as it would turn out. Although I didn't know it at the time, Stephanie—yes, the same Stephanie whom we earlier glimpsed briefly in the tea-room of the Grafton Picture House—was already spoken for, and our trysts, few and sweetly melancholy as they were, had to be held in venues well away from the public gaze of Dublin, one of the world's most pruriently vigilant cities.

There was a secret place, she told me, that very few people seemed to know about, and where hardly anyone ever went. We visited the Gardens for the first time on a hurried but never-to-be-forgotten lunchtime date; she brought sandwiches and I, hopefully, a bottle of wine that in the event turned out not to have the desired effect—it was cheap and nasty, and anyway Stephanie was too canny a girl to let herself be led into tipsiness by a beady-eyed young brute with not much more on his mind than the one usual thing.

It was early autumn that day, and under a Poussin sky the trees were the dry-olive shade they take on before the final turn, and made a wistful, dreamy rustling high up above us in the bird's-egg-blue air. Before we settled to our picnic Stephanie insisted on showing me round what she considered to be practically her private domain.

I see us there, as clear as the September day itself, pacing the gravel paths beside the pleasingly unkempt lawns, under those restive trees, in search of a secluded place in which to settle ourselves. Here are the fountains, there is the archery range—and, oh, smell that fragrance wafting to us from late blossoms in the rose garden over the way! Supposedly there was a maze, too, she said, but she had never been able to find it. I held her hand. I was wasting my time, she said, wasting my time; and yet she smiled, and allowed her hand to rest in mine. It is out of such moments, commonplace yet plangent, that the past, the longed-for past, assembles itself.

The Iveagh Gardens, naturally, have their own past. They are first mentioned publicly in the mid-eighteenth century as Leeson's Fields. The land was leased to a developer, John Hatch, who gave it as the garden to a house on Harcourt Street built for the chief justice, John Scott, Lord Clonmell, an enthusiastic drunkard quaintly and no doubt accurately known as Copper-faced Jack.* In 1810 Clonmell House was sold and the space behind it was opened to the public as Coburg Gardens. In the early 1860s the site was purchased by Benjamin Guinness, scion of the brewing family. Benjamin, like so many of the Guinnesses then and now, was of a philanthropic cast, and seems to have lent or perhaps leased the land to the splendidly named Dublin Exhibition and Winter Garden Company, to be the pleasure grounds of the Dublin Exhibition of 1865.

The Exhibition Building, which later on would become University College Dublin and then the National Concert Hall, was considered at the time, *pace* Christine Casey, to be a magnificent edifice. It had an adjoining Winter Garden, a vaulted hall of glass and steel the structural stability of which was tested, according to Casey,

---

* Appropriately enough, there is now a nightclub in Harcourt Street named after him, from which, no doubt, more than one clubber staggers of a night, if not copper-faced then certainly shit-faced.

by 'monitoring hundreds of running workmen, 600 marching men of the 78th Highlanders and the rolling of several thousand cannonballs'.

Meantime Benjamin Guinness had purchased numbers 78-81 on St Stephen's Green and combined them into a fine mansion, Iveagh House—now the Irish Department of Foreign Affairs—and, the Exhibition being over, reclaimed the gardens and commissioned the landscape architect Ninian Niven—how resonant were the names in those lost days!—to furnish a new design for them, combining French and English landscaping styles. In 1908 Benjamin Guinness's son Edward, 1st Earl of Iveagh, donated the gardens to University College, which in Edward's honour renamed them Iveagh Gardens.

By the time I came to them the Gardens, now backing both the National Concert Hall and the Department of Foreign Affairs, had fallen again into happy neglect.

The Gardens are not large, being I imagine about the size of a football field. Features include, so the guidebooks tell me, rustic grottoes and a cascade, two fountains, woodlands and a wilderness, a rosarium, an American garden, archery grounds, rockeries and rooteries—I confess I am not quite sure what this last-named might be—and a maze. The possibility of this mysterious maze in particular pleases me, since in all the times I have visited the Gardens I, just like Stephanie long ago, have never succeeded in finding it. Now, it is one thing to be lost in a maze, but that there should be a maze one cannot find seems to me a truly marvellous thing, a conceit straight out of a wonder-tale by Borges. Thinking it over, I entertain the fancy that if there were indeed to be an afterlife—horrible possibility—there would be worse ways of enduring it than in an endless Borgesian circular search for this ever-elusive garden feature within a garden.

In the mid-1990s the Office of Public Works instituted a renovation of the Iveagh Gardens. Good work was done, I suppose, but I preferred them in their prelapsarian dishevelment of the old days, when I went there wistfully a-courting of my girl-who-was-not-my-girl. Parks—and let us grant that this little plot aspires successfully to the condition of a park—are ambiguous, indeed at times sinister, places. Remember Antonioni's *Blow-Up*? Who, having seen that film, will forget the agitated soughing of trees on the soundtrack while David Hemmings's fashion photographer is developing a roll of snapshots taken in a London park and discovering that he has captured on film what seems to be the commission of a murder? And then certain habitués of parks seem always to be *up to something*. One can come upon a figure huddled on the grass, eyes shut fast, cheek on hand, clothing all awry, and walk on with the uneasy question in one's mind: *Was he sleeping, or . . .?* This faint hint of pervading menace is part of the pleasure of parks, just as much as the fountains and the flower beds and the scent of autumn roses.

And then there are the statues. I am sorry to say that there is a great paucity of them in Iveagh Gardens. The twin fountains are manned by a facing pair of identical muscular angels with disproportionately large hands—for lifting up the righteous from the clutches of the forces of evil?—and on concrete plinths there stand a couple of vague, less-than-life-sized female figures, both of them

noseless, their complexions marred by lichen, gazing downwards in what seems weariness and unrelievable dejection. 'A few cast gods and naiads remain,' Christine Casey sadly observes. It was not ever so: 'An account of 1872 described figures of the Spirits of the Land, a figure of Erin seated on shamrocks, figures of the Four Provinces and of St Patrick.' Somehow I do not feel compelled to mourn the passing of these paragons. A modern figure, in bronze that is at once shiny and muddy, of the tenor John McCormack stands in a holly bower, mouth agape, like that of a baby bird demanding to be fed. He looks so terribly sad, posed there and giving his mute all to the unheeding greenery roundabout. But, then, he would not be happy either, I suspect, in the Jardin du Luxembourg, dwarfed by the figures of so many of his heroic *confrères*.

My most recent visit to the Iveagh Gardens was in the company of my younger daughter. She was sixteen at the time. I had brought her with me to show her a place precious to me, where I was once sweetly and unhappily in love. However, I discovered, to my great surprise, that she knew the place well. Her boyfriend, it turned out, lived nearby, and it was here, on weekdays after school, that they would come to walk, and be together, discussing the great issues of the day, finding out about each other, learning to grow up. As she told me this, in her not unkind though offhand way—the young are entirely deaf to the joggling palpitations of an aged heart—I had a sense of the magical timelessness of such places, and of the uses to which we put them. We change, we age, we stay or move away, and in time we end. The park, however, endures. It is a thought, I think, to comfort, if only by a little, the most distressed of hearts.

· · · · ·

The Delahayes, my Stephanie's family, were Protestants. They were said to be of Huguenot stock, and indeed they might have appeared before me got up in perukes and doublets-and-hose and I would not have been in the least startled, so exotic and archaic a phenomenon did they seem to me. Before I was introduced to the family, I had come in contact with very few real, live Protestants, and certainly had never conversed with a gathering of our separated brethren as I did with the Delahayes, on what was, or at least was pretended to be, an equal footing. They lived in Fitzwilliam Square, which was at the time, and may still be, the Dublin version of Harley Street, the almost exclusive preserve of pinstriped medical consultants, the 'five-guineas-a-go men', as my Aunt Nan dismissively referred to them. One of these fashionable doctors had his 'rooms' on the ground floor of the Delahayes' house, while they occupied the upper storeys and the basement.

They were a sprawling family. Stephanie was the only girl, but there were five brothers, from a toddler called Gervaise—it seemed to me absurd that such a short, stumbling, snotty-nosed creature should boast so heraldic-sounding a name—to a burly bruiser of twenty or so, with a truly frightening set of teeth that gleamed whitely when he grinned, resembling, so I thought, some sort of primitive implement of the Eskimos for trapping fish or fighting off seals. His name was Thomas, but the family nickname for him was Tiddler, because of his giant size, naturally.

The Delahayes in general went in for calling each other by faintly derisive pet-names. Mrs Delahaye, bird-like, with a slight stoop and dyed hair as shinily black and brittle-seeming as shellac, bore the rather lovely name of Lavinia, although the children for some reason called her Mags, while I never heard her husband address her as anything other than 'Old Girl'. Mags chain-smoked Gitanes— her 'gaspers', as she grimly called them—so that the house smelt throughout like a French *bistrot*. She was also, as it turned out, a secret drinker, or secret from me, anyway, in the beginning. Her tipple, I eventually discovered, was Gordon's gin mixed with, of all things, that egg-nog-like stuff made by Bols, the comical-sounding Dutch distiller; it was the colour of beaten egg-yolk and had the consistency of phlegm—Advocaat, that was the name; it has just come to me.

Thomas—Tiddler—I clearly recall, and Gervaise I remember too, though less clearly, but the middle three brothers have melded in my recollections of them into a sort of multi-headed, half-formed monster, and therefore I shall here refer to them collectively as Cerberus. They teased Stephanie without mercy—they delighted in calling her 'Steph', knowing how much she hated the diminutive— and never lost an opportunity of embarrassing her before the rest of the family, and me. I recall a Sunday lunch when someone had accidentally let fall some drops of raspberry jam on one of the dining-room chairs, and Cerberus joined its voices together to denounce my poor darling for having 'bled on the bloody furniture again'. My presence in the household, short-lived though it was, Cerberus greeted with hand-rubbing delight. They would mimic my culchie* accent—I hadn't thought I had one—and would endeavour to engage me in po-faced discussions of bucolic matters such as turnip-snagging or muck-spreading, about which I knew as little or less than they did. I heartily loathed Cerberus, which only made the beast lift its multiple snouts and bay all the more delightedly.

The father of the Delahayes was big and bluff and red-faced, and almost entirely bald, save for a rather endearing fringe of prematurely grey curls, like a fallen-down halo, that gave him the look, to my eye, of one of the jollier and less debauched Renaissance popes. His name was Victor, and Cerberus, of course, called him Vicky, though only behind his back, for he did not know his own strength, and the cuffs he enthusiastically dealt out to all the boys— he doted on Stephanie and would not even raise his voice to her— had enough power behind them to make even the hulking Tiddler wobble on his pivot.

Delahaye *père* was a former rugby player—a 'rugger-bugger', as he liked to say, with a huge laugh—and had been capped for Ireland numerous times in international matches. It was never quite clear

---

* It is said the word 'culchie', which is how Dubliners witheringly refer to country people, derives from Kiltimagh, an entirely blameless town in County Mayo. How a corruption of its name should have become synonymous with yokelhood no one can explain, though the derivation is taken for a fact, by Dubliners, at least.

to me what he did for a living, though I knew it was something connected with the law; I suppose he was a solicitor, or perhaps a barrister. Evidently he was successful at his work, whatever it was, for the family, raucous, ragged and chaotic though it might be, was obviously well-off, in an unostentatious way. Their moneyed status was evident in the way they ate—groceries from Findlaters, wine from Mitchell's, foie-gras from Smyths on the Green—and the way they dressed: Brown Thomas and Switzers in Dublin, and, in London, Harrods, which Stephanie and her mother visited twice-yearly to purchase their summer and winter outfits.

The family went on foreign holidays, too, a thing almost unheard-of then, certainly among the kind of plain people I came from. The places they holidayed in were odd, however: Guernsey, for instance, and the Isle of Man; I wonder now if Mr D had offshore bank accounts, and used these jaunts as a cover for tending them.

It was an extremely noisy household, and it's a mystery how Mr O'Grady, the ground-floor gynaecologist, and his patients put up with the racket. There was the frequent thunder of young feet on the stairs, an incessant flushing of lavatories; there were the hoots of Cerberus's laughter and the furious shrieks from Stephanie when she was being teased. Mr Delahaye used to sing, too, in a booming bass, as he pottered about in his voluminously flapping corduroy trousers and his sleeveless canary-yellow jumpers. He favoured arias from Gilbert and Sullivan, and obscure music-hall ditties—'If It Wasn't For the 'Ouses In Between', 'Boiled Beef and Carrots', 'When Father Papered the Parlour'—forgetting half the lyrics and always gratingly out of tune.

Mrs Delahaye, poor half-sozzled Mags, was the only quiet one in the house. She confined herself to a continuous soft vague twittering that was not exactly speech, but seemed rather a sort of distracted, incomprehensible disavowal, as if she imagined there were people all round her all the time asking her questions she could not answer or even understand. My presence seemed to baffle her, and every time she encountered me she would give a tiny start, which she would hasten to cover up with a remote, faintly pained smile, putting her head to one side in an attitude of apologetic haplessness. Maybe she thought I was yet another of her sons, whom she had unaccountably misplaced and who now had been mysteriously returned to her. She rarely addressed me directly, but when she did she would pluck a name for me at random, as if out of a card file in her head, James, or Joseph, or Gerald, and once even, fantastically, Jasper.

Despite the rackety if sometimes heartless good humour of the house, there was, behind it, a barely perceptible feeling of apprehensiveness, the nature or source of which I could not identify until, many years later, I read in Harold Nicolson's diaries for 1934 an account of his calling on James Joyce one day at the Joyces' flat—'as stuffy and prim as a hotel bedroom'—in the rue Galilée in Paris. It is a wonderful vignette, a model of its kind. Nicolson thought Joyce's 'the most lovely voice I know—liquid and soft with undercurrents of gurgle', but he found the man himself a distinctly odd creature.[*]

---

[*] He had 'the impression of a very nervous and refined animal—a gazelle in a drawing room'.

The atmosphere in the tiny room where they met, along with Joyce's adult son Giorgio, was strange and strained, and observing the two men, father and son, Nicolson felt distinctly 'that they were both listening for something in the house'.

That, I realised, was how it had been at the Delahayes'. They all rushed uproariously about, the sons scuffling and shouting and the father booming his silly songs, while at the same time, secretly, everyone was listening, listening intently. I presume that what the Joyces feared hearing were the cries of the great man's poor demented daughter Lucia; in the case of the Delahayes it must have been Mags who kept them on tenterhooks. I never heard her so much as raise her voice, but perhaps she was on her best behaviour when I was there, though likely at any moment to rend the air with wild, inebriated ravings.

There was usually, besides me, another visitor—I almost said interloper—in the house, an exceedingly pale young man who dressed always in black—black suit, black tie, long black overcoat and sometimes, sinisterly, a pair of strangler's soft black leather gloves. His name was Fitzsomething—Fitzmaurice or Fitzmorris, I fancy— although Cerberus had dubbed him Pierrepoint, after Pierrepoint the hangman. He was tall and exceedingly thin, with a prominent hooked nose, and he wore spectacles with very fine wire rims. He smoked cigarettes in a holder, like Father Lee, and now that I think of it, he did have in general a priestly mien. His fingernails, which he grew very long, were nicotine-stained to a shade of amber, and were never entirely clean. He always seemed to manage to be there before I arrived, and always was gone before I left, although I do not remember ever seeing him leave. When I pressed Stephanie to know who he was she screwed up her mouth and lifted one shoulder in a dismissive shrug and said, 'Oh, he's a sort of cousin.'

Mags was not at all vague in her dealings with Pierrepoint, as she was with me, and pressed upon him all manner of treats. I would arrive and there he would be, seated at his ease in an armchair in the front drawing room, by the big bay window that looked out on the square, with a glass of sherry or port and a slice of plum cake on a little table beside him, his gloves folded on the arm of the chair, his tie narrowly knotted but never askew, two identical stars of light from the window gleaming on the toecaps of his shiny black brogues. He was perfectly polite to me, polite but distant, although I always felt there was the suspicion of a smirk about his pursed and femininely pink little rosebud of a mouth.

As residents, the family had access to the railed-off garden in the middle of the square. On sunnier days—the air was steadily dimmening as the autumn progressed—Stephanie would take down an enormous iron key, big and heavy enough to bludgeon to death Professor Plum in the parlour, from the last hook on the coat-rack behind the front door, and we would cross the road and open the ancient little gate, so rickety it seemed held together only by immemorial layers of glittering knobbly black paint.

Here was another of my beloved's secret places, even more intimate and certainly more deserted than Iveagh Gardens.

We would walk along the narrow pathways, under the drooping

trees and between the damp bushes, the rubbery leaves of which were always sprinkled with diamond drops, even on dry days— but, then, in that season it is always after rain. How thoughtful and expectant everything looks in autumn, much more expectant, certainly, than in spring. Not even Keats caught the stillness and the stealthy tumult of the dying season with such poignant precision as Philip Larkin does in a little poem from 1961, which, inexplicably, he chose not to publish, and to which he did not even give a title:

> *And now the leaves suddenly lose strength.*
> *Decaying towers stand still, lurid, lanes-long,*
> *And seen from landing windows, or the length*
> *Of gardens, rubricate afternoons. New strong*
> *Rain-bearing night-winds come: then*
> *Leaves chase warm buses, speckle statued air,*
> *Pile up in corners, fetch out vague broomed men*
> *Through mists at morning . . .*

And autumn, not spring, and much less summer, is the season of love. Stephanie Delahaye I loved, for those few weeks at the end of September and the beginning of October, loved her helplessly, with a kind of agonised tenderness.

What did we talk about, as we paced the four sides of the square, or sat on one of the coldly damp iron benches? I have forgotten; what do the young talk about? I do recall having an argument with her about Pascal, something to do with a passage I had read in the *Pensées*, which she insisted I had misunderstood. This gives the impression that we were both wonderfully well-read, when really all we were doing, I see now, was showing off to each other our spurious knowledge of a subject of which we were almost entirely ignorant. Pascal!

We had met for the first time at the Lantern Theatre when it was in residence in a basement in Merrion Square, just round the corner from Mount Street. Dublin was a city of tiny theatres in those days. There were the Eblana, in the basement of a bus station, and Deirdre O'Connell's Focus in a mews off Pembroke Street, and the Gas Company Theatre, though that was way out in Dún Laoghaire—one entered through the dimly illumined showrooms, weaving one's way among the ghostly, off-white forms of somehow resentful-seeming cookers of all shapes and makes—and the Pike, of course, in Herbert Lane, founded by Alan Simpson and Carolyn Swift. It was the Pike that in 1955 staged the first uncensored English-language production of *Waiting for Godot*—in London the lord chamberlain had insisted on changes and deletions—and Behan's *The Quare Fellow*.

Notoriously, in 1957 the Pike was raided by the Gardaí, who had been informed that the play being produced, to mark the inauguration of the Dublin Theatre Festival, *The Rose Tattoo* by Tennessee Williams, contained passages that were 'objectionable', and that if the production went ahead, Simpson and Swift would be liable to prosecution. The play did go ahead, and next day Simpson was arrested and charged with putting on 'an indecent and profane performance for profit'. There were protests, in Dublin and internationally, and after an absurd legal wrangle that was not resolved until the following year, the charges against Simpson were withdrawn. Few in Dublin had any doubt that the original complaint against the production of *The Rose Tattoo* had come directly from the Archbishop's Palace: once again the dead hand of John Charles McQuaid had fallen upon the artistic life, or half-life, of Dublin.*

Years afterwards, in the early 1970s, I met Alan Simpson at the launch in the Bailey of Christy Brown's *Down All the Days*—this was the publishing party my editor David Farrer had come over from London to attend—and asked him about the affair. Simpson, suave and elegant as always, gave me what seemed a long, florid and detailed account of everything that had happened; so drunk was he, however, that I could not understand a word he said, and therefore missed out on the inside story. But, then, everyone was drunk at that party—the drinks bill for the evening was to be for years a legend in the British publishing world.

The play that was on at the Lantern the night I met Stephanie was either Shakespeare's *Julius Caesar* or *Titus Andronicus*, I can't remember which. I do remember that it was a wonderful performance, despite or perhaps because of the cramped conditions in the 'auditorium'—

---

* In 1958 there was further interference in the Dublin Theatre Festival, when Sean O'Casey was asked to make changes to his play *The Drums of Father Ned* and promptly took the play out of the festival; then Bord Fáilte—yes, the Tourist Board—forced the withdrawal of *Bloomsday*, a stage adaptation of *Ulysses*. Beckett had given permission for productions at the Pike of *All That Fall* and *Endgame*, but on 27 February 1958 he wrote to Carolyn Swift:

> I am withdrawing altogether. As long as such conditions prevail in Ireland I do not wish my work to be performed there, either in festivals or outside them.
> If no protest is heard they will prevail for ever. This is the strongest I can make.

people in the first two or three rows were liable to be sprayed with spittle whenever an actor stepped to the edge of the stage to deliver a particularly impassioned speech. At the interval I climbed the steps and stood by the railings and smoked a cigarette. It was not quite night yet, and a phantasmal whitish mist was wreathed among the trees in the square, and I could feel a clammy dampness on my face and on the backs of my hands.

Half the audience was on the pavement along with me, looking vague and displaced, as theatre audiences always do during the interval. The only one of them I took any notice of was Stephanie. She was slight, with an almost boyish figure. Her shoulder-length dark hair was parted in the middle—I noted with an inexplicable pang the paleness of the skin where it glimmered in the parting. Her nose was slightly fattish, though I found it entirely lovable; her eyes had a slight upward tilt at the outer corners, which gave her a faintly Oriental aspect, especially when she leaned forward and lowered her head. She seemed to be on her own, which in itself was striking—in those restricted times 'nice' girls never went anywhere without an escort, except to confession. I offered her a cigarette—thinking uneasily of the lame whore in Mount Street— but she smiled with lips pressed shut and shook her head. She did not smoke, she said. She was eighteen. She lived nearby. Oh, yes? So did I. After this half-hearted canter we lapsed into silence, and Stephanie looked down frowningly, making half-circles on the wet pavement with the toe of her shoe. Then she drifted away from me, with that deliberately distracted, bland expression that girls put on when they are extricating themselves from a purposeless encounter.

When the play was over, and we were coming up the basement steps into the night's liquid darkness, I wriggled my way forward through the crush until I was beside her. I asked if I might walk her home. She said her brother was coming to meet her. No one was waiting at the top of the steps. Stephanie hesitated uncertainly, avoiding my eye. 'He's always late,' she murmured, more to herself than to me. I suggested that we should go along together, and meet him on the way. She shrugged, said nothing, and we set off. We exchanged not a word, until at the corner of Fitzwilliam Street Tom Tiddler loomed up before us, huge and square-shaped in a brown duffel coat. He greeted me with a grin—he really was a decent fellow—showing off those alarming teeth of his. I told him my name, and he told me his. Stephanie looked at neither of us, and walked on. Tiddler raised his eyebrows at me, I said nothing, and he grinned again and turned and followed her. It was hardly an auspicious beginning. All the same, I was in love. As I watched Stephanie and her gigantic brother disappear into the mist, I felt like Humphrey Bogart in *Casablanca*; or, better still, Marcello Mastroianni in Antonioni's *L'Eclisse*.

She had not given me a telephone number, nor had she told me where she lived, so how did I find her again? That piece of the mosaic is missing. But find her I did.

I cannot think what the family made of me. The fixed convention of the day was that a boy and a girl could not simply be friends, and everyone knew—everyone except me—that I was not Stephanie's boyfriend. So who was I? My floating presence would hardly have been allowed in a Catholic household, or else we would all have had to pretend that I was there because of Stephanie's brothers and not because of Stephanie.

Yet we went, the two of us, on what I, at least, considered to be dates. I took her to the pictures, where she let me hold her excitingly cool slender hand, and to tea at the Grafton Picture House; once even we braved the Palace Bar, where the barman frowned at us but served us two glasses of beer anyway. We walked in St Stephen's Green, and sat amid the damp bluish shadows of Fitzwilliam Square. We stood by the canal at Lower Mount Street Bridge and watched a heron hunting there beside the lock; I was awestruck by the clean sharp dangerous lines of the thing, the long bill like a lovingly fashioned ceremonial blade. She showed me the Iveagh Gardens. I told her I loved her, but she closed her eyes and smiled, with her lips pressed shut, which is the way she always smiled, and shook her head. All the same she let me kiss her, dryly, chastely. She had an intoxicating smell, as of rose petals soaked in slightly soured milk.

Then came the day when I found an envelope, delivered by hand, waiting for me on the mat inside the door of the Mount Street house. I didn't recognise the handwriting, yet I knew whom the note was from. My throat had thickened before I had even begun to read it. *No use . . . so sorry . . . I really liked . . . maybe we could . . .* Strangely, she had signed it 'Steph', that version of her name she knew I knew she hated. Steph—what did it mean? Was it a way of distancing herself from me? A wave of sorrow and self-pity washed through me, and I thought I might be sick.

For a moment, blinded in a hot red mist, I hated her.

• • • • •

I encountered her again on two occasions. The first time I had no more than a glimpse of her from afar. Autumn had turned into a hard winter, and in the middle of December a heavy snow fell, and everybody was happy because the weather was so definitively bad that we were relieved of having to talk about it. I was in Grafton Street. This was before that narrow, delicately undulating thoroughfare had been ruined by pedestrianisation—one of those words that is as ugly as its meaning—and buses were sashaying down the middle of the road between frozen ruts of sooty snow, and women on the pavements were slipping and shrieking and clutching on to their menfolk's sleeves, and there was a general sense of hilarious misrule. It was mid-afternoon and already the Christmas lights were glowing brightly in the frost-laden air, and the waft of roasting coffee beans from the doorway of Bewley's Oriental Café was a soft brown breath of warmth.

She was the one I spotted first, of course, on the far side of the street—my poor heart gave a sort of anguished quack at the sight of her—and only after some moments did I realise who it was she was with. They were arm in arm, and Stephanie was leaning into the hollow of his shoulder like a skiff cleaving to the lee shore of a sheltered bay. She was wearing galoshes—people still wore galoshes, then—and a brown coat with an ugly fur collar. Her head was bare. She

was smiling, saying something, and he was nodding in the po-faced way that he did. It was Fitzmaurice or Fitzmorris, whose first name, I have just this moment remembered, was Desmond. Desmond; ah, yes, the gentleman caller who was always in the house before me and always gone before I left. He was in his long black narrow overcoat, going along stiff and stately with a mincing tread—his was not so much a walk as a progress—looking insufferably self-satisfied, and suddenly I saw, for the first time, the remarkable resemblance he bore to—oh, my sainted aunt!—Éamon de Valera, yes, the smug and saintly hawk-nosed Dev. And I saw, too, that *he* it was, Fitzwhatever, who had been the boyfriend all along, while I had been—what? No one. Nothing. A redundant and probably annoying dropper-in, tolerated only out of good manners. Small wonder that Cerberus had quivered so in three-headed mirth whenever I was about!

I drew my neck into the collar of my coat and hurried on.

The following summer I saw her again, and this time we spoke. It was one of those dreamy June evenings when the low sun hovers on the horizon, seeming unwilling to set, and the sky is flecked with pure white mares' tails and the far-off pale-mauve mountains seem as insubstantial as stage-flats.* We met in Fitzwilliam Street, at exactly the spot where she had walked away from her brother and me that first night after the performance at the Lantern. She was pushing her baby brother Gervaise in a big black pram; in fact he was

---

* Trieste is the only other city I know of where mountains seem to jostle ethereally at the far end of almost every street.

no longer a baby, but a large, ruddy-faced, top-heavy and, to my eye, somewhat brutish toddler—he was going to be the spit of his father, that was plain. This time we were on the same side of the street. We saw each other from some way off, and both of us hesitated, although there was no way of avoiding each other unless we were to turn on our heels and walk off in opposite directions. I stopped. She stopped. She smiled, in a deliberately clownish, lopsided fashion, giving a rueful little shrug, as if to say, *Well, I suppose we were bound to meet some time or other*. We spoke for no more than a minute or two, though it seemed far longer to me, and surely to her, too. What agonies we go through on such unlooked-for occasions! She seemed tired, and her eyes had an uncharacteristically dull, evasive look, with dark smudges beneath them. I asked after the family. She turned aside, squinting off towards those distant dream-blue mountains, and sucked in her lower lip. Her mother, she told me, had died, just after Christmas. Poor Mags! The fags and the booze had got her at last. I said I was sorry. Stephanie shrugged again, lifting one shoulder and letting it fall. Silence rose up between us, like the chill water in a well. Gervaise, impatient at this delay, was giving me a soiled, sideways glare. 'I'd better . . .' Stephanie said, and her voice trailed off. That's how things end in real life: a shrug, a child's impatience, and the unutterable enormity of love pressing hotly behind one's breastbone like a hot lump of lead.

I wonder if she married Fitzwhatsit. I wonder if she had a happy life, or at least a not unhappy one. Strange to think of her being somewhere, at this moment, doing something. Stranger still to think of her perhaps not being here; of her not being anywhere.

7

Time Regained

W E HAVE BEFORE US TODAY, Cicero and I, what the
newspapers in their showbizzy star-struck days used
to refer to excitedly as a whirlwind tour. We shall start
at the Blessington Street Basin—or Bason, as the original spelling
had it. It is a reservoir, officially the Royal George Reservoir, built
in the first decade of the 1800s to supply drinking water to the city,
and which continued to operate until the 1970s. The water came
from Lough Owel in County Westmeath, delivered along a spur of
the Royal Canal that has since been filled in to make a handsome
tree-lined walkway beyond the Basin at right angles to Blessington
Street. By the end of the 1860s the reservoir was too small to serve
the city adequately, and other arrangements were made, although

the Basin continued to supply the Jameson and Powers distilleries.

We start our approach from the foot of Blessington Street, stopping to look admiringly up the low rise towards the Basin's handsome gates, just inside which stands a mock-Tudor cottage that reminds me of a Kylemore Bakery chocolate log. There are some fine Georgian and early-Victorian houses still standing in the street, and not a few of them are inhabited, their burnished windows revealing, to the inveterate nosy-parker, all the appearances of muted middle-class *bien-être*. We walk round the pool, in the centre of which sits an overgrown, spiky, porcupine-like little island, and is home to a good stock of wildlife, including swans and ducks and some distinctly proprietorial pigeons, which squat fatly on an iron rail and watch us with beady malevolence, as if to say, *Shove off—we were here first.*

The area around the reservoir was from the start designated as a public park, and was a fashionable place of promenade for Victorian gentlemen and their ladies. Cicero chuckles at the thought. By the time he knew it, in the late 1950s, 'you wouldn't be doing much promenading in these parts, I can tell you'. As we come out through the original, sturdily handsome doorway* into Blessington Street

---

* 'Look at that granite,' Cicero says, fingering the stippled stone blocks of the doorframe. 'Bush-hammered, that effect is called. Masons with little sharp hammers, *tap tap tap*. They knew how to handle material in those days.' As in the house in Henrietta Street, here he makes me run my palm over the surface of the big steel door, knobbly and warmish under centuries of black paint, to feel the weight and quality of the material, the sureness of the workmanship. He does love a well-crafted artefact, whether it's a table he once showed me, by Moore's of Dublin, *c.* 1760 — satinwood, demi-lune, tapered leg with collar, the whole thing as lithe and poised as an antelope—or a big functional iron door such as this one. He is, as Thomas Hardy hoped to be, a man 'to notice such things'.

Park, which occupies the filled-in canal, he exclaims with surprised pleasure at the eclectic mixture of dwellings, from working-class cottages through nineteenth-century two- and three-storeyed middle-class houses to an ultra-modern wooden 'studio' that fits in perfectly with its surroundings. If this is gentrification, we agree, then please, let us have more of it—lots more.

Cicero points to an original cobbled laneway, and bids me mark the parallel slate tracks along either side, designed to ensure smooth running for the wheels of coaches and carts. The cobbles are missing in a patch at the foot of the lane, and have been replaced by a perfunctory dollop of tarmac. Cicero is incensed. 'How can they *do* that?' he cries. 'Those missing cobbles should have been replaced by modern substitutes, in keeping with the design and layout—no attempt at making it look like the original: repairs should always be honest, and announce themselves as what they are. That's how it should be done.' He glares at the bumpy tarmac, shaking his head. 'Vandalism, that is,' he says. 'Publicly sponsored vandalism.'

And at once I am transported back to an occasion years ago, I can't remember how many, though I know it was before the Crash of 2008. That day Cicero took Seamus Heaney and me to lunch in a restaurant in Upper Pembroke Street, hard by Fitzwilliam Square of blessed Delahaye memory. At the time Seamus was ill after a stroke, and the occasion, though as funny and entertaining as were all occasions that were celebrated in the vicinity of Seamus, was touched with a tender melancholy, a kind of shadowed sweetness. Cicero, who is fascinated by the creative process, quizzed Seamus

as to how a poet goes about making a poem, and Seamus, while unable to supply a comprehensive answer—who knows how a poem is made?—was as considerate and courteous as ever.

We came out of the restaurant into a blustery, mercurial afternoon—I can't recall if it was spring or autumn, for in my memory it could have been either—and Cicero drew our attention to the pavement, which had gaps among the flagstones—the flags of Dublin pavements are as variegated and in their way as intricately handsome as Dublin brick—that had been filled with, of course, tarmac. On the spot Cicero came up with a plan to persuade the city authorities to undertake a general repair of Georgian footpaths all over the city, using contemporary Wicklow granite. I think the scheme was to be funded by money from the National Lottery, or maybe he envisaged a public subscription. I believe he even wrote out and sent the proposal to the City Council or the Office of Public Works. It was an excellent scheme, and would have added much to the texture of the city's historic squares and boulevards, but of course nothing came of it, for shortly afterwards Lehman Brothers crashed about our ears, and we all went broke.

'Och,' Seamus said to me afterwards, when we had parted from Cicero, 'but he's a great man for the plans.'

$\bullet \ \bullet \ \bullet \ \bullet \ \bullet$

From the Basin we drive down to North Great George's Street, one of the most elegant and most nearly intact of the city's Georgian sites, imposingly loomed over at the top end by Belvedere House, which was built in 1786 for the egregious George Augustus Rochfort, 2nd Earl of Belvedere, and used as a Jesuit school since the early 1840s—it was Joyce's alma mater.[*] We are hoping to stop for a cup of coffee at the Cobalt Café, which occupies the ground floor of one of the grander houses on the street, but it's closed, as it was the last time I called there. The Cobalt is among the more eccentric and colourful of the city's watering-places. Next time, perhaps . . .

We are on our way to the Rotunda[†] Hospital, in Parnell, formerly Rutland, Square. The Rotunda is called after the adjoining building in the complex—which would eventually become the Rotunda Cinema, later renamed the Ambassador—and is the oldest working maternity hospital in the world. It was founded by one of Irish history's truly admirable figures, Bartholomew Mosse, surgeon and 'man-midwife', who in 1745 opened a lying-in hospital in a converted house in George's Lane near Smithfield market, the first such institution in the British Empire. A few years later, with only five hundred pounds in his pocket, he took out a lease on a large tract of land at the north end of Sackville Street, the present-day O'Connell Street, and began building a new hospital, to a design by Richard Cassells, who died, however, a few months before building

---

[*] A friend of mine many years ago encountered one of Belvedere College's retired teacher priests, and in the course of a conversation with him unwisely mentioned Joyce's name. This provoked a heavy silence, which the reverend father broke at last by clearing his throat, looking at the ceiling, and murmuring: 'Ah, yes, Joyce. Not one of our successes.'
[†] Was ever a maternity hospital more aptly named?

commenced. The grand edifice was originally planned to close the vista at the end of Sackville Street, but Mosse and the ubiquitous Luke Gardiner quarrelled, with the result that Gardiner built what is now Cavendish Row as a continuation of Sackville Street, thus forcing Mosse to move his hospital some way to the side.

Mosse was not only a medical pioneer but also a highly successful impresario. In the land behind where the hospital would stand he had set up a combined pleasure garden, known as the New Gardens*—a visitor from London pronounced it the equal of Vauxhall Gardens—which included a concert hall and coffee house. Mosse used the accumulated earnings from the garden, some eight thousand pounds, a great sum of money in those days, along with a grant of six thousand from the government, to build the hospital, of which he was the first master. The New Garden was not only a commercial but also a social success, with the result that by the end of the 1700s Rutland Square was one of the most fashionable areas north of the river—in the 1790s, Maurice Craig informs us, 'it was the residence of eleven peers, one peeress in her own right, two bishops and twelve Members of Parliament'.

Cicero has arranged an appointment with the present master, Professor Fergal Malone, who receives us hospitably and shows us around the older parts of the hospital, for the splendours of which

---

* The Rotunda complex also includes the Gate Theatre, leading Maurice Craig, with characteristically subdued wit, to observe how the Rotunda 'permanently cemented' the 'close alliance between obstetrics and entertainment'.

he has an infectious enthusiasm. We see the original entrance front, which I thought rather grand but about which Christine Casey in her book on Dublin is decidedly sniffy, dismissing Cassells's design — she calls him 'Castle' — as 'characteristically leaden'. The hall is a not very large cubic space of simple design, which must have offered welcome reassurance and warmth to expectant mothers entering there. In those times the babies of the better-off were delivered at home, under the care of man-midwives such as the good Dr Mosse, but he had instituted his hospital for the specific purpose of treating the poor folk of the city.

Buried in the very depths of the hospital is the chapel, described by Christine Casey as 'the most eloquent [eighteenth-century] church interior in Ireland', and also, delightfully, as 'the incongruous belly-jewel of a sturdy matronly form'. It is a double-height square space with stained-glass windows and a wrought-iron gallery on three sides. We enter through a short passageway, pressed upon to right and left by working maternity wards, in each of which are twelve beds occupied by twelve mothers and their babies. The contrast between the dim quietude within the chapel and the clamour and movement of a busy maternity hospital outside is enough to make one's head spin.

In the good old days, Cicero can tell me, Guinness used to supply a free daily snipe of stout to each patient in the hospital. Into the mouths of babes . . .

Cicero has a personal connection with the Rotunda, apart from the fact that he was born here. On the wall of one of the inner corridors there hangs an oil portrait of Dr Walter Wade, another surgeon and man-midwife, who practised in the city towards the end of the eighteenth century. The picture was presented to the hospital, as a brass plaque proclaims, by Cicero himself; he bought it for a few pounds at auction many years ago. 'Strange to think,' he says, as we stand contemplating the portrait, 'that this will be hanging here, with my name on it, long after I'm gone . . .' A sombre yet comforting thought, especially in this palace of parturition.

In the portrait Dr Wade is holding in his fingers, somewhat oddly, it might seem, a pink rosebud. The incongruity is dispelled when Cicero explains that Wade, professor of botany of the Dublin Society—founded in 1731, and now the Royal Dublin Society— campaigned for the setting up of a public botanical garden, and in 1790 formally petitioned Parliament to that end. In 1795 the government bought from the poet Thomas Tickell* his house and grounds in Glasnevin and donated them to the Society. Wade became the first director of the National Botanic Gardens, and it was there that Cicero and I were bound next.

As we drove up Glasnevin Hill he told me that it used to be known as Washerwoman's Hill, since it was the place where in former times women did their laundry on the banks of the Tolka river. Jonathan Swift lived here, opposite the Model School, and so did another

---

* One wonders if it was this Tickell Beckett was thinking of when in his early novel *Murphy* he invented the figure of 'Austin Ticklepenny, Pot Poet, From the County of Dublin'. Though unkind spirits have suggested that in fact Ticklepenny is a spiteful caricature of Austin Clarke.

writer, the Englishman Joseph Addison, a friend of Swift's and a member of the Irish Parliament in the early 1700s; Cicero has a handsome, engraved medallion with Addison's portrait, dating from the time of his Irish sojourn.

He confides to me that it was in the Botanic Gardens that he got his first kiss. I ask for details, but he shakes his head. He also recalls that when he was a teenager the Botanic Gardens — the 'Bots' — used to grow marijuana plants, and that on more than one occasion he surreptitiously garnered the makings of a spliff or two.

The present director of the Gardens, Matthew Jebb, was away that afternoon, but we were welcomed by the curator, Paul Maher, who invited us into his office in a secluded corner within the grounds. The room, low-ceilinged but ample, seems less like a botanist's headquarters than, oddly but charmingly, a sea-captain's cabin, due mainly to a proliferation of complicated antique instruments, including a primitive brass barometer. There is also a bookbinder's cast-iron paper press, the presence of which even Paul cannot account for. He shows us many things, including an enormous volume containing daily weather records, written out in flawless copperplate handwriting, that go back to the earliest days of the Gardens. He also has on display a baobab nut, brought to him from Africa by his botanist daughter; it is as big as an elongated coconut. He shows us a photograph of himself standing under a baobab tree that is the size of a three- or four-storey house. He would tell us a million things, and show us another million, had we, and he, the time.

I think I have never met a man so content in his work and so passionately committed to all aspects of it as Paul Maher obviously is. He tells us that back in the 1980s he took leave of absence for three years to run his own garden-design business. Was it a success? we ask. It was, he answers, but the fact was he 'missed the plants' and had to return to the Gardens and his beloved work and his wonderfully cosy office. A fortunate man.

The afternoon is moving on, and we should be moving with it. First, however, I must pay a visit to one of my favourite buildings in all the world.

The Great Palm House of the Botanic Gardens was built in 1884, an airy confection of glass, steel and wood; its predecessor was blown down in gales and this one was built by hardy Scots in the town of Paisley and transported here, God knows by what means. It was meant to last, which it did, until the Millennium, by which time it had fallen into such disrepair that it had to be closed to the public, not to reopen until five years later, after being thoroughly restored.

Regarded with a sceptical eye it looks like nothing on earth, and as for the things inside it . . . Elephantine is the word that springs — or lumbers, rather — to mind when we first enter, and find ourselves in the midst of so many enormous trees crowding together in a hot mist, their huge auricular fronds inclined towards us as if entreating a word of consolation, or at least of explanation. How, they seem to ask, did they come to be here, jostling together silently in this vast, glistening space, so far from the shrieking jungle? Dominant and hugely helpless, can they ever have been small — can they ever have

been saplings? They are not disproportionate to us: no, it is we who are disproportionate to them, a pair of Lilliputians confronted by a crowd of Gullivers, planted there in the sand with their hairy thick old socks around their ankles.*

In this greenly aqueous air we have an under-sea sense, and as we pace beneath the unswaying leaves we seem to ourselves languorously afloat in a sluggish, tepid stream. There are walkways up there, high above our heads, among the upflung fronds, narrow, perforated metal platforms that must surely lead to diving boards; we would not be surprised should there come a sudden splash followed by a swimmer streaking down in an arc and skimming past us, making fish-mouths, with his hands—his palms!—pressed together above his head.

And there is so much glass, panes and panes of it, both flat and curved, and all opaque with mist. The summer sunlight enters from all sides, making the drenched air glow and turning it to a turbid gold. We think of the people, grave frock-coated gentlemen, dundrearied, elaborately moustached, who designed and put up this perfectly calibrated, utterly mad caprice, this gay gazebo. Who says the Victorians were dull? Now here it stands, a stately pleasure dome for the city to delight in, to be awed by, to be frightened of, a little. Surely we cannot be all bad, as a species, if we could think it right and necessary to erect this airy bubble and fill it with these uncanny and utterly endearing monstrosities.

---

* Amelia Stein has taken wonderful photographs here—see her splendid book *The Palm House*, published by Lilliput Press.

And, look, there's Wittgenstein's commemorative plaque. I wonder what he made of the palms. Perhaps, so deep in thought, he didn't even notice them.

· · · · ·

And still the day's mad round continues. We hurry off next to Ringsend* and the south Docklands, and in particular to that point, at the end of the road on which Cicero lives, where the Dodder, the Grand Canal and the Liffey all merge. Here are three magnificent locks, the Westmoreland, the Buckingham and the Camden, opened in 1796, an occasion of pomp and ceremony that is celebrated in William Ashford's painting *The Opening of Ringsend Docks, Dublin 1796*, which can be seen in the National Gallery of Ireland. The locks are still operated, by lock-keepers George Brierley and his son Stephen, although the last cargo barge plied the canal in 1960.

We pause to admire these elegant granite troughs, but our true destination is a nearby pair of dry docks, even more elegant, though sadly disused now and hidden within a makeshift enclosure overgrown with grasses and weeds. They are shaped somewhat like old-fashioned bathtubs, tapering towards one end, and are constructed in stepped blocks of granite — the whole effect puts me

---

* See Appendix II.

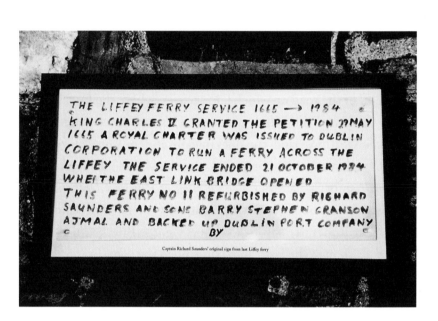

THE LIFFEY FERRY SERVICE 1665 → 1984
KING CHARLES II GRANTED THE PETITION 29 MAY
1665 A ROYAL CHARTER WAS ISSUED TO DUBLIN
CORPORATION TO RUN A FERRY ACROSS THE
LIFFEY THE SERVICE ENDED 21 OCTOBER 1984.
WHEN THE EAST LINK BRIDGE OPENED
THIS FERRY NO 11 REFURBISHED BY RICHARD
SAUNDERS AND SONS BARRY STEPHEN GRANSON
AJMAL. AND BACKED UP DUBLIN PORT COMPANY
BY

Captain Richard Saunders' original sign from last Liffey ferry vaguely in mind of Greek amphitheatres. In the larger of the two docks there languishes the rusting hulk of a cargo ship, the *Naomh Éanna*, which squats disconsolately in the stagnant water, like an ungainly, wounded water-bird.

Cicero explains to me the unhappy history of Dublin's canals. They were built, with much labour and at enormous expense, to join the capital in the east to the Shannon in the west, and thus open both coasts and the midlands to trade. However, since Ireland had no coal and no overseas colonies, and therefore no industrial revolution, the huge profits that had been foreseen by the businessmen and manufacturers behind the canals scheme never materialised. Then came the railways, which meant goods could be delivered from one side of the country to the other in hours rather than the days it took by water, and that was virtually the end of the canals. The result was financial ruin for a great many speculators, large and small. *Plus ça change* . . .

However, Cicero, the man of plans, has a vision for the future of the two dry docks. He means to drain, refurbish and cover them with a translucent, sky-blue weatherproof roof, making of them one vast space, to be called the Agora, after the ancient Greek word for a city assembly area, which will be open to all. Here music events will take place, markets will be held, skating rinks will operate, pop-up shops will pop up, there will be late-night movie shows, monster céilís, and more — in other words, the entire area will be revitalised. It is a daring vision, exciting, forward-looking and, according to Cicero, entirely feasible, given a little encouragement from the city authorities and

a deal with the owners, Waterways Ireland. He describes it all to me as we walk back along Hanover Quay, past the old Raleigh bicycle factory, which has been converted into the European headquarters of Airbnb. Capitalism comes in many forms . . .

Directly at the back of Cicero's house is a wide stretch of water, supplied by the Grand Canal before it meets the Liffey. As we emerge on to the waterside, a renovated Liffey ferry is docking. The ferry, the last one in existence, was salvaged and restored by master mariner Richie Saunders. Richie is going to take me for a spin around the basin—it might be 8 December again, and I a child looking forward to a treat. We board, and Richie describes how the ferries used to carry dockers to and fro across the river by the hundreds, in the days before the docks, like everything else, became automated. As we pass by a narrow street leading to the Google headquarters—high-rising capitalism again—Richie chuckles as he tells me how he and his mates often moor here on Thursdays and go ashore to collect their pensions from the post office nearby.

We sail underneath a bridge, built askew to the road above, and view the exquisite masonry of the arch, in which all the stones are cut and fitted on the bias. How many times have I passed over here without an inkling that this magnificent example of the stonemason's art was hidden underneath? So much of the world is concealed from us.

'We could go to the Shannon from here,' Richie says wistfully. What a trip that would be!

· · · · ·

We are at the end of our tour, indeed of our tours, and it's time for a parting glass. We drive into Poolbeg Street—this will be my last fling, for now, anyway, in the little red roadster—and stop at Mulligan's. This fine old pub was established first in 1782 in Thomas Street, and moved to its present location in 1854. It is a quiet afternoon, and we sit at a little table just inside the door. The sun is shining, and dust motes drift in the air. I feel like Odysseus come home at last to Ithaca, but with all in order and no usurping suitors in need of slaughtering. I feel—yes, I feel at home. Cicero and Dublin between them have, I realise, granted me the freedom of the city. I offer a toast just to being here—*'because being here is much'*—and smile, inanely, I fear, at the sunlight in the doorway. A shadow falls there, and who should come in—no such thing as a coincidence—but my eldest son, my firstborn, who is a man now, middle-aged and taller than I am. He is on his way home from work, and has stopped in for a pint, just like my father used to do, all those years ago, in another world, in another age.

O time, O *tempora*, what places we have been to—and where will you take me yet?

Appendix I

Have you ever wondered what is under those enormous Georgian buildings? Here is Maurice Craig's account of what one of James Gandon's masterpieces, the Custom House on the north bank of the Liffey, rests upon:

> Gandon decided not to use piling. Instead he pumped out the space in a cofferdam [look it up], levelled it off, laid down a quantity of cut heath, and on top of this a huge grating of Memel timber [keep that dictionary open] of section one foot square. He then filled in the interstices with good stock brick in a mixture of pounded roach lime and mortar, and covered the whole with four-inch fir planking. Then came a course of rough mountain granite, embedded in which was an iron chain four inches by two and a half, the collars run with lead and the bars covered with a cement of wax, resin and stone dust. Regular granite courses brought the work to ground level. Under

the rest of the south front the grating was covered with
Dublin calp. Time has proved the soundness of Gandon's
construction, but during the building he was subjected
to some frivolous criticism by amateur architects who
came to gape down into the black oily depths . . .

Cicero tells me that Gandon, when he was building the Custom
House, encountered so much passionate opposition that he would
not venture on to the site without a sword. Kevin Roche, the Irish-
American architect who designed the Conference Centre just
downriver from Gandon's masterpiece, was greatly tickled by the
story, so much so that Cicero presented him with an eighteenth-
century sword forged in Dublin, which still hangs in the New York
offices of Roche Dinkeloo Associates.

Appendix II

I can never hear the name of Ringsend, 'that gem that sparkles on the Dodder', without thinking of my favourite of all Dublin ballads, 'Johnny Doyle', or, 'The Forgetful Sailor'. I used to think it was written by that great singer, the late Frank Harte, but I am informed by Nicholas Carolan, Director Emeritus of the Irish Traditional Music Archive, that in fact it is the work of James—Jimmy—Montgomery, the first Irish Film Censor, who held the post from 1923 to 1940. A devout Catholic, he declared that as Censor, 'I take the Ten Commandments as my code.' Thanks for saving our parents' generation from the moral depredations of Hollywood, Jimmy.

Here are the lyrics of the song:

Johnny Doyle, or, The Forgetful Sailor

You sons of Dan O'Connell's line, give ear unto my doleful ditty,
It's all about a sailor lad, whose birthplace was in Dublin city.
My song is just to demonstrate a story with a pious moral

That starts around by Carlisle Bridge and ends up on the Isles of Coral.
A schooner sailed from George's Quay, for foreign parts one sultry season,
And on the shore, a maiden stood and cried like one bereft of reason.
'Oh Johnny Doyle, my love for you is true but full of deep contrition
For what'll all the neighbours say about me in this sad condition?'
The capstan turned, the sails unfurled, the schooner scudded down the Liffey,
This damsel gave a piercing shriek, she was a mother in a jiffy.
The vessel passed the harbour bar and headed out for foreign waters,
To China, where they're very wise, and drown at birth their surplus daughters.
Now years and years have passed and gone, and Mary's child is self-supporting,
And Mary's heart is fit to break when this young buck goes out a-courting.
And so says she, 'On one fine day, he'll go and leave me melancholy;
I'll dress meself in sailor's clothes and scour the seven seas for Johnny.'
She shipped on board a pirate bold that raided on the hot equator,
And with these hairy buccaneers there sailed this sweet and virtuous creature.
The captain thought her name was Bill, his character was most nefarious.
Consorting with this heinous beast, her situation was precarious.
'Twas in the Saragossa Sea, two rakish barques were idly rolling,
And Mary on the middle watch, the quarter deck she was patrolling.
She calmly watched the neighbouring ship, then suddenly became exclaimant,
For there upon the gilded poop stood Johnny Doyle in gorgeous raiment.
And now they're back in sweet Ringsend, the gem that sparkles on the Dodder.
He leads a peaceful merchant's life and does a trade in oats and fodder.
By marriage lines she's Mrs Doyle, she runs a stall of periwinkles,
And when Johnny hears one's on the way, his single eye with joy it twinkles
And now their family numbers ten, and Mary's heart sings like a linnet,

For Johnny's calmed that wild young buck that stretched her patience to the limit.
They're happy now in sweet Ringsend, no more they'll sail for foreign waters,
For Johnny Doyle, his hands are full, with five strong sons and five sweet daughters.

Acknowledgements

The following books were of much help to me in the writing of *Time Pieces*:

Dublin 1660–1860, by Maurice Craig, Cresset Press, 1952

The Buildings of Ireland: Dublin, by Christine Casey, Yale University Press, 2005

Georgian Dublin: The Forces that Shaped the City, by Diarmuid Ó Gráda, Cork University Press, 2015

Remembering How We Stood, by John Ryan, Lilliput Press, 2008

Prodigals and Geniuses: The Writers and Artists of Dublin's Baggotonia, by Brendan Lynch, Liffey Press, 2011

Warmest thanks to Raymond Bell, Stephen Brierley, George Brierley, Nicholas Carolan, Ciara Considine, Margaret Crean, Rita Crosbie, Vonnie Evans, Joan Hanly, Helen Hanly, Paul Maher, Professor Fergal Malone, Helena Gouveia Monteiro, Richie Saunders, Louisa Stoney, and the staff of Pearse Street Library.

Fragments of this book first appeared, in different form, in *City Parks: Public Places, Private Thoughts*, created and edited by Catie Marron, with photographs by Oberto Gili, HarperCollins, 2013, and *Sons+Fathers*, edited by Kathy Gilfillan and published by the Irish Hospice Foundation, 2015.

Permissions
Acknowledgements

The author and publisher would like to thank the following for permission to use material in *Time Pieces*:

Excerpt from *The Newton Letter* by John Banville (Picador, 1982) reprinted with kind permission of the publisher.

'Lines Written on a Seat on the Grand Canal, Dublin' by Patrick Kavanagh is reprinted by kind permission of the Trustees of the Estate of the late Katherine B. Kavanagh, through the Jonathan Williams Literary Agency.

Excerpt from 'Next, Please' by Philip Larkin (*The Less Deceived*, 1977) reprinted with kind permission of Faber & Faber Ltd.

'And now the leaves suddenly lose strength' by Philip Larkin (*Collected Poems*, 2003) reprinted with kind permission of Faber & Faber Ltd.

Image Captions